Moustafa Gadalla was born in Cairo in 1944. He graduated from Cairo University with a Bachelor of Science in civil engineering in 1967. He immigrated to the U.S.A. in 1971 and continued to practice engineering as a licensed professional engineer and land surveyor. He is an independent Egyptologist who spent most of his adult life studying, and researching scores of books about Egyptology, mythology, religions, the Bible, languages, etc. He often lectures and writes articles about ancient Egypt.

He is the author of four internationally acclaimed books about ancient Egypt. He is also the chairman of the Tehuti Research Foundation, an international, U.S.-based, non-profit organization, dedicated to ancient Egyptian studies.

Other Books By Author

Historical Deception
The Untold Story of Ancient Egypt
ISBN: 0-9652509-5-4 (pbk.), 352 pages
$19.95 Pub. in 1996 by Bastet Publishing

Pyramid Illusions
A Journey to the Truth
ISBN: 0-9652509-7-0 (pbk.), 192 pages
$11.95 Pub. in 1997 by Bastet Publishing

Tut-Ankh-Amen
The Living Image of the Lord
ISBN: 0-9652509-9-7 (pbk.), 144 pages
$9.50 Pub. in 1997 by Bastet Publishing

Egyptian Cosmology
The Absolute Harmony
ISBN: 0-9652509-1-1 (pbk.), 160 pages
$9.95 Pub. in 1997 by Bastet Publishing

Although the author and publisher have tried to make the information as accurate as possible. Prices, schedules, and conditions of places mentioned, can change either way. Therefore, both the author and publisher accept no responsibility for any loss, injury, or inconvenience sustained by any person using this book.

Readers who have comments, corrections, or ideas they would like to see reflected in the next edition of this book, are invited to submit them by mail, fax, or email, to the addresses noted on the last page. Significant contributions will be rewarded with a free copy of one of the books listed on the order form at the end of this book.

EGYPT

A Practical Guide

Moustafa Gadalla

Tehuti Research Foundation

EGYPT
A Practical Guide

by Moustafa Gadalla

Published by:
>Tehuti Research Foundation
>Post Office Box 39406
>Greensboro, NC. 27438-9406, U.S.A.

All rights reserved. No part of this book may be reproduced or transmitted in any form or by any means, electronic or mechanical, including photocopying, recorded or by any information storage and retrieval system without written permission from the author, except for the inclusion of brief quotations in a review.

Copyright © 1998 by Moustafa Gadalla, All rights reserved.
Printed in the Egypt, 1998

Cataloging in Publication Data

Gadalla, Moustafa.
   Egypt: A practical guide / Moustafa Gadalla. -- 1st ed.
   p. cm.
   Includes bibliographical references and index.
   Preassigned LCCN: 98-72254
   ISBN: 0-9652509-0-3

   1. Egypt--Guidebooks. 2. Egypt--Civilization.
3. Egypt--Antiquities. 4. Pyramids--Egypt   I. Title.

DT45.G34 1998   916.204'55
              QBI98-11157

Manufactured in Egypt
Published 1998

Table of Contents

Table of Contents — 5

Introduction — 9

1. **Demographic Information** — 10
   Geography - Weather - Language - Population & People
   Religions - Economy - Agriculture - Education - Names
   of Places

2. **Cultural Tips** — 17
   Orientation and Getting Directions - Greetings & Civilities - Tipping & Gratuities - The Smoking Egyptians
   Tourist Police - How Egyptians View Tourists - Women
   Travellers - Photography - No Intimacy in Public Places
   Unposted Prices - Littering the Streets - Treatment of
   Animals - Tour Guides - Talking to Egyptians

3. **Planning Your Travel** — 22
   When to Go - What to See - Who to Plan With - How to
   Get Information - Tourist Offices Abroad - ETA Offices
   in Egypt - How to Get There - Where to Stay - What to
   Pack - Health & Vaccinations - Visas & Documents -
   Student Discounts - Crime in Egypt

4. **Arriving & Departing** — 34
   Visas at Point of Entry - Airport Hustlers - Customs -

Registration - Antiquities Permits - Travel Permits - Vaccinations - Return Ticket - On Departure

5. Getting Around Egypt — 37
What to Wear - What to Carry With You - Calling Home Time - Newspapers & Magazines & Maps - Radio & Television - Coping with the Environment - Getting Sick in Egypt - Money Exchange & Credit Cards - Nile Activities - What to Eat - Places to Eat - What to Drink - The Night Life - What to Read - What to Buy - Where to Go Shopping - Business Hours - Transportation Between Cities - Transportation Within Cities

6. Historical Information — 58
Pre-Dynastic Era - The Glorious Pharaonic Era - Ptolomaic Era - Roman & Byzantine Rule - Arab Rule Turkish Rule - British Occupation - Independent Egypt

7. Understanding Ancient Egyptians — 64
Religion - The Neteru (gods/goddesses) - Animal Worship - Symbolism & Neteru - Their Language - The Per-aa(Pharaoh) - Sacred Texts(Their Writings) - Temples - The Obelisks - Monument Usurping - The Pyramids of Egypt - Why the Stone Pyramids Are Not Tombs - The All-Egyptian Story (Isis & Osiris) - Egyptian Art (The Cube) - The Egyptian Calendars

8. Cairo & Vicinities — 84
Greater Cairo Area - Points of Interest (Pharaonic Sites, Christian Sites, Islamic Sites, Modern Sites) - The Giza Plateau - Memphis - Saqqara - Dahshur - Meidum - The Nile Delta - The Suez Canal

9. Middle Egypt — 128
Beni Hasan - Mallawi - Hermopolis (El Ashumnein) - Tuna el Gebel - Tehuti, Master of Khmunu - Tell el

Table of Contents

Amarna - The Akhenaton Story

10. *Luxor/Thebes*(Ta-Apet) — 138

East Bank - Luxor Museum - The Apet and Feast of the Valley Festivals - Accomodations - How to Get to Luxor - Luxor Temple - Temples of Karnak

West Bank - Valley of the Kings - Valley of the Queens - The Hatshepsut Commemorative Temple - The Hatshepsut/Tuthomosis III Real Story - The Ramesseum Commemorative Temple - Seti I Commemorative Temple - Ramses III Commemorative Temple (Medinat Habu) - Colossi of Memnon & The Vanished Temple - Tombs of the Nobles - Village of the Workmen (Deir el Medina)
The 42 Negative Confessions

11. Sites North of *Luxor*(Ta-Apet) — 178
Dendera(*Enet-ta-ntr*) - Abydos(*Abtu*)

12. Valley of the Upper Nile — 186
Esna - El Kab(*Nekheb*) - Kom el Ahmar(*Nekhen*)
Edfu - Kom Ombo

13. *Aswan*(Sunt) & Abu Simbel — 194
Aswan(Sunt) - How to Reach Aswan(*Sunt*) - Accomodations - The Unfinished Obelisk - Nile Feluccas - Elephantine (*Yebu*) Island - Sehel Island - Botanical (Kitchener's) Gardens - The Rock Tombs - The Temple of Kalabsha - The Aswan Dam - The High Dam Auset(Isis) Temple of Ancient Philae - The Sites: Philae and Agilka - Auset(Isis) Beloved of All

Abu Simbel - The Temples - The Relocation of Abu Simbel Temples - Transportation and Accomodations

14. Alexandria Alexandria - Points of Interest - Accomodations & Transportation	**208**
15. The Mediterranean Coast	**212**
16. The Egyptian Sahara Oasis El Fayoum Oasis - Bahariya Oasis - Farafra Oasis - Dakhla Oasis - Kharga Oasis - Siwa Oasis	**214**
17. The Red Sea Hurghada (Water Activities - Submarine Ride) - Safari Trips - Accomodations and Transportation - Safaga - El Qosseir	**222**
18. Sinai Hammam Fara'un(Suez Gulf) - Water Activities - Sharm el Sheikh & Na'ama Bay - Ras Mohammed - Tiran Island - Dahab - Nuweiba - Taba - St. Catherine's Monastery - Mt. Sinai - The Bedouins - Overland Exploration - El Arish - Transportation to Sinai	**226**
Glossary	**232**
Selected Bibliography	**244**
Index - General	**246**
Index - Maps	**255**

Introduction

"Now, let me talk more of Egypt for it has a lot of admirable things and what one sees there is superior to any other country."
— *Herodotus, 500 BCE*

"...in Egypt all the operations of the powers which rule and work in heaven have been transferred to earth below...it should rather be said that the whole cosmos dwells in [Egypt] as in its sanctuary..."

"There will come a time when ... the gods will return from earth to heaven; Egypt will be forsaken, and the land which was once the home of religion will be left desolate, bereft of the presence of its deities."
— *Ascleptus III (25 BCE), Hermetic Texts*

Even though much of what Herodotus witnessed has been ruined by the cruelty of later generations, his statement is still valid to this day. Today's Egyptians have abandoned their ancient heritage for a mostly Moslem Arabic-speaking nation. Happily, they have maintained their friendly, hospitable, and warm characteristics.

Em Hetep (meaning *In Peace*, in ancient Egyptian language).

Moustafa Gadalla

1. Demographic Information

Geography

Egypt is located in the northeastern corner of Africa. Almost square in shape, it covers an area of 1 million sq km (390,000 sq mi). Its longest distance north-south is 1,085 km (675 mi) and widest distance east-west is about 1,240 km (775 mi). More than 90% of the country consists of desert area. Only about 5% of the vast country is inhabited, along the banks of the Nile. This fertile Nile Valley is a strip, 11-15 km (7-9 mi) wide.

To the east of the valley is the Eastern (Arabian) desert - a barren plateau bounded on its eastern edge by a high ridge of mountains, and the Red Sea. Sinai, east of the Suez Canal, includes Mount Catherine, Egypt's highest mountain, reaching 2642m (8720ft).

To the west of the Nile Valley, is the Western Desert - a plateau with plush oases scattered about a vast desert.

The Nile flows through Egypt from south to north. Lower Egypt is thus the north and Upper Egypt is the south. That's because the country slopes downhill toward the Mediterranean Sea. Going upriver means heading south to Luxor and Aswan, and going down the Nile means heading north towards Cairo and Alexandria.

North of Cairo, the Nile splits into several tributaries, the main two being the Rosetta and the Damietta branches. The valley becomes a delta, a wide green fan of fertile country-

Demographic Information

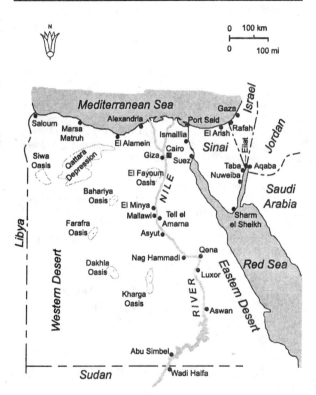

side, some 15,500 sq km (6000 sq mi) in area.

The northern coast, west of Alexandria, extends for hundreds of miles, with brilliant white-sand beaches. Some have been, or are being, developed as resorts.

Weather

Autumn and winter are the ideal seasons to visit Egypt when mild weather prevails, temperatures vary between 16°C (60°F) and 27°C (80°F). Evenings are cool. Prolonged rain is uncommon, except in Alexandria in the winter, but showers may fall elsewhere between October and April.

During April, an occasional hot sand wind blows which can make sightseeing less enjoyable.

The summer months are hot, 27-38° C (80-105° F); however, the air is dry and humidity low. The relative humidity, in Egypt, ranges from 30-60%.

In Alexandria, on the Mediterranean Sea, the months of December through February are rainy and cold. October to April represents the best time, with water temperatures of 16-22°C (60-70°F).

Sinai has unique weather. The desert is typically hot during the day and cold at night, but the mountains can be chilly, even during the day.

Language

Arabic is مصر مركز الحضارة Egypt's official language. However, most Egyptians understand and speak English and French. In larger towns, the foreign visitor will encounter no difficulty in communicating with the people.

Arabic is written from right to left. Its alphabet contains 28 letters. The Arabic sentence above reads "Egypt: Centre [of] Civilization".

Population & People

In 1998, Egypt's population totalled 65 million. About 90% of Egyptians are concentrated in the fertile Nile Valley, and live in 5% of the country's territory - 44% in urban areas and most in some 4,000 villages. Cairo, Egypt's capital, has 14 million inhabitants, and Alexandria, the country's second largest city, has a population of 5.5 million.

The population increases at a rate of one million every ten months. As a result, 50% of the population is now under 18 years of age. As a consequence, the public services and infrastructure are under a great strain.

The Egyptians are outgoing, warm and have a distinct sense of humor. They have respect and a liking for foreigners.

Religions

Approximately 85% of the population of Egypt are Moslems. Most of the rest are Christian Orthodox, who belong to the Coptic Church. There is also a small Jewish community, still residing in Egypt.

Islam

Islam means '*submission*'. The Moslems believe in the one God, Allah, AND that Mohammed is his prophet. *Allah* is an Arabic word, meaning "*Who has everything*". According to Islamic traditions, Moslem followers are encouraged to spread the word, even by force if necessary.

Moslems have five main acts to follow, as directed by the Koran (Qur'an), the Moslem's holy book. These Five Pillars of Faith are:

1. The Moslem must publicly declare that 'There is no God but Allah and Mohammed is his Messenger'. These two go hand in hand. You can't have one

without the other.

2. The Moslem must pray five times a day, at specific times between dawn and early evening. A person can pray anywhere. Only male Moslems are required to attend the Friday noon mass prayer at the mosque.

3. Moslems are required to give a certain percentage of their wealth to *zakah*(charity), for the needy, and to further the cause of Islam.

4. Moslems must fast from dawn to sunset, during the Islamic lunar month of Ramadan.

5. At least once in a lifetime, the Moslem must make the haj, or pilgrimage to Mecca, if at all possible.

Throughout Egypt, you will notice the mosques' thin towering minarets, some as high as 80m (260ft). These are used by the mosque officials, known as *mu-azzen*, to announce the call to prayer. Faithful Moslems follow the call and may stop what they are doing, go off into another room, or to the mosque, and begin their prayers.

Mosques are built so that they point towards Mecca. When a Moslem enters a mosque, he removes his shoes, and washes himself in a certain way, then commences to pray.

Prayers are a pre-defined set of routines, to be followed in the same order each time. The worshipper faces the direction of Mecca, bows, kneels, places his palms on the ground, then his nose and forehead. He then stands, and repeats the cycle for a specific number of times.

Visiting Mosques - You can only visit mosques designated by the Ministry of Tourism as 'tourist sites', and not during times of prayer. You must dress modestly (men - no shorts, women - no shorts or sexy clothing). Use common sense and respect. Remove your shoes or 'rent' the shoe coverings available at the entrance to the mosque.

Egyptian Coptic Christianity

In 333 CE, Christianity became the religion of the Roman Empire. A short time later, the Empire split. Egypt became part of the Eastern (or Byzantine) Empire. Dioscurus, the patriarch of Alexandria, refused to accept the Byzantine Christian doctrine. He believed that Christ is totally divine, and that it is blasphemous to consider Him human. Since that time, Egyptian Christians have been referred to as Coptic Christians.

'*Copt*' is derived from the Greek rendering for an *Egyptian*. The Arabs, after 640 CE, labeled non-Moslems as *Copts*. As a result, the term '*Coptic Church*' took on a diferent meaning by the 7th century.

Judaism

Egypt currently has fewer than 500 Jews, mostly elderly, scattered through Alexandria, Cairo, and El Minya, near the capital city of Pharaoh Akhenaton. There were more than 80,000 Jews in Egypt until 1948. After the independence of Israel and the animosities in the region, their number dwindled to a trickle.

Economy

Before the 1952 revolution, Egypt's economy depended mainly on agriculture. Egypt is expanding its inhabitable land by using new irrigation methods, and encouraging people to relocate to the new land reclamation areas.

Today, tourism is the main source of revenue, and there are many exports, such as oil, textiles, canned foods, and cotton goods. The Suez Canal is also a sizeable source of income, with about 50 ships a day paying fees.

Agriculture

Egypt continues to produce high quality agricultural products, such as rice, sugar cane, fruits, vegetables, and cotton. The Nile Valley has highly fertile soil, and you will see the results, if you chance upon a Farmers' Market, or notice the enormous, colourful fruits and vegetables in small vendors' carts everywhere.

Education

The education system is composed of four stages - primary (years 1-6), preparatory (years 7-9), secondary (years 10-12), and university. Primary education is mandatory and is extended to children between the ages of six and twelve. Education in Egypt is provided free to all Egyptians. However, it is highly competitive at the university level, to get the institution and major of your choice.

Names of Places

In Egypt, you will find that a place, or an ancient name/reference, may have several names: its Pharaonic (original), Greek rendering, which got popularized worldwide, and Arabic, which was given to it after the 640 CE invasion of Egypt. Throughout this book, the real, legitimate name, i.e. ***Pharaonic***, will be shown in ***bold italics***. Other common names will be shown in *regular italics*. Nobody likes his/her name arbitrarily and disrespectfully changed.

2. Cultural Tips

Orientation and Getting Directions
When asking for directions in Egypt, don't ask for street names. Ask for a specific location/building. Many people may give directions, even if they are not sure (just being too helpful!). Thank the person, and as soon as s/he is out of sight, ask another person to confirm. If you get different directions, ask someone else. Repeat this process until you reach your destination.

Greetings & Civilities
It is considered rude not to greet people when you meet, leave, etc. Greet others in any language. It is your demeanor that counts more than your words. Sincerity is important - a patronizing attitude does not fool anybody.

Tipping & Gratuities
It is a sad fact that there will be many people (adults and children) you may encounter, who will ask for unearned tips, referred to as, *baksheesh*. It is best not to reward such behaviour by succumbing to their pleas. Just say NO, firmly.

As for the people who do indeed provide a service for you (with your consent), they deserve your tips. Coins and small bills in a separate pocket, are handy for a quick tip, and assure decent service the next time you show up.

The Smoking Egyptians

Many Egyptians smoke. Smoking cigarettes is a status symbol with most of them. Even if smoking is restricted in public places, they will smoke anyway. If it bothers you, mention nicely but firmly that you have lung problems, and smoking makes you ill.

Tourist Police

Tourist Police are a special force provided by the government to promote and assure a friendly, civil tourism business/environment. They wear normal police uniforms - black in winter, white in summer - with an armband reading *Tourist Police*. They speak at least two foreign languages, and you will find them at the popular tourist locations. If you find yourself in difficult a situation, such as a difference of opinion over price, etc, mention the words "Tourist Police!", and if that doesn't resolve it, go and find one. Also, any uniformed policeman will help you.

How Egyptians View Tourists

Egyptians think that tourists are very rich; that they have fulfilled all their life expectations, and still have excess money to travel to Egypt. Such an understanding leads them to inflate prices, beg, or expect money. They believe that other countries have perfect laws and systems, and as a result, these tourists can afford to travel. They don't, or don't want to, know that one in the West must work hard and abide by the rules, and sacrifice other luxuries, to save up money to travel. They also forget that in many cases, the Egyptians have a higher expectation in life than Westerners. While those in

Cultural Tips

the West shop at garage sales, purchase generic brands, and do their own laundry, Egyptians insist on nothing but the best brand, and pay somebody else to wash and iron all their clothes. Egyptian marriages are usually postponed until enough money is saved up to purchase apartments and top-of-the-line furnishings - every last detail, right down to the last piece of crystal, as well as expensive jewelry for the bride, and enormous wedding receptions.

Even though you will always be treated hospitably and cordially, under the surface, Egyptians think that there is a Western conspiracy against them and Islam, to keep their living conditions below that of other countries.

Egyptians also believe that non-Islamic countries have no morals. Foreign movies, magazines, and TV programs are reinforcing this assertion, since they are full of sex scenes where affairs are accepted as a matter of routine, with no consequences. The result is, that a foreign woman may become a sex target.

Women Travellers

The woman traveller needs to be aware of the Egyptians' image of Western women, and take some basic steps to avoid any misunderstandings or uncomfortable situations. Dress modestly - be comfortable, not sexy. Act politely and professionally. Avoid direct eye contact with Egyptian men, unless you know them. Ignore obnoxious comments, or persistent, overly-friendly overtures. Be firm, never apologetic or diplomatic. "I came here to see your beautiful country, and nothing else." Maintain space around yourself, especially in crowded areas. A good idea, is to wear a wedding band.

Fortunately, even though Egyptian men can be persistent, actual physical threats and violence are non-existent.

If you follow the advice above, with your attire and attitude, you will find most Egyptians to be very hospitable, kind, peace-loving people, who want, more than anything else, for you to have a wonderful time in their country.

Photography

The best times to take photographs of any outdoor sites, are early morning and late afternoon. Use a lense filter to cut glare and reflection off sand and water; and to protect your lense.

You can take photos of the interiors of mosques, temples and some tombs. Using a flash inside sites of antiquity, is absolutely forbidden, because it fades the artwork, but you can photograph tomb interiors without a flash (use a fast-speed film), if you obtain a special permit beforehand.

If taking photos of anything other than tourist and scenic sites, check first. Egyptian children love to have their pictures taken. Not all adults like to be photographed, especially covered women. Therefore, it is best to receive their prior consent.

Egyptians don't like picture-taking of the less attractive sights of Egypt, such as garbage or beggars.

No Intimacy in Public Places

Egyptians frown on public displays of affection and intimacy.

Unposted Prices

In most places, prices are not posted. Ask others about the going prices, to be prepared, and bargain accordingly.

Littering the Streets

Is is a sad state of affairs, but the Egyptians have a bad

habit of littering their streets and public buildings with garbage.

Treatment of Animals

Dogs and cats are allowed to roam the streets and sites of antiquities freely. These dogs are generally not territorial.

You may be shocked and dismayed at how Egyptians hit their donkeys and horses as they run in the streets. Look the other way. Your protest will make them laugh, which will only infuriate you more.

Tour Guides

Tour guides are university graduates. At times, they may blend facts with fiction, to make the subject more interesting. Their knowledge of Egyptology is very "orthodox", especially as it relates to the ancient Egyptian beliefs. Listen with a grain of salt.

They can be very helpful to tell you of prices, etc. However, many of them are known to take tourists to shops where they get a special commission.

Talking to Egyptians

Egyptians are very friendly and eager to engage into conversation. Ask for their opinions, but listen with a grain of salt. Many of them have their own personal agendas.

Frequently, they are simply interested in practicing their English, and speaking with people from other countries.

Egyptians are very tolerant and understanding of the fact that people from other countries may have different customs or beliefs. Basically, as long as the visitor isn't disrespectful or arrogant, other differences will go unnoticed.

3. Planning Your Travel

When To Go

The height of the tourist season in Egypt is their winter - from mid-October to May. Summers (May to mid-October) in Egypt are very hot, especially in Upper Egypt (Luxor and south), but because it is a dry, desert heat, it is fairly tolerable. If you choose to travel in the summer (the lower cost is a great incentive), try to keep your sight-seeing earlier in the morning, before the hottest part of the day.

The sandstorms (khamsin) are nasty hot sandstorms that blow variably, usually February to April. Storms rarely occur more than once a week, so your schedule won't be thrown off too badly. They may interfere with some sightseeing plans in the desert. Within the city of Cairo, when a sandstorm occurs, it gets a little more dusty, but everyday life continues.

Because the majority of Egyptian adults fast between sunrise and sunset, during the lunar month of Ramadan, shopping and sightseeing become more difficult. Shops close in the afternoon or have shorter daytime hours. There are some exceptions for businesses that cater mostly to foreign tourists.

The starting date of Ramadan slips forward 10 to 12 days each year on the Western calendar. For the next few years, Ramadan will be in December and January.

What to See

Packaged tours are your best way to get a good flavour of Egypt, particularly if it is your first visit. A popular package is a two week visit, including time in Cairo to visit the pyramids of Giza, Saqqara, and the museum, as well as a 3-4 day Nile cruise between Luxor and Aswan.

For the people with an interest in the underwater sea life, an excursion to the Red Sea or Sinai is very popular. Some of the best underwater sea life in the world can be found in both places.

Who to Plan With

It is best to work with a travel agent, for all your travel arrangements: the flight, airport pick-ups, accommodations, internal travel, and day-to-day excursions and activities.

There are innumerable travel agents, big and small. Use word of mouth and references before choosing one of them.

Check with the Egyptian Tourist Authority,
> http://touregypt.com

for their latest list of Egyptian travel agencies.

How To Get Information

You can get information via the internet, from the Eyptian Tourist Authority - http://touregypt.com - for the latest tourist information. This is a vast on-line resource about Egypt, which is constantly updated.

The Rediscover Ancient Egypt website,
> http://www.egypt-tehuti.com

provides much information about ancient Egypt.

You can also get information from the offices of the Egyptian Tourist Authority (E.T.A.) in Egypt and abroad. They have maps of Cairo and Egypt, as well as brochures on various sites around the country.

Tourist Offices Abroad

Austria
Agyptisches Fremdenferkersamt. Elisabethstrasse - 4 / 5 / 1. Opernringhof. 1010 Wien. AUSTRIA. (Tel: 431 587 6633, Fax: 431 587 6634)

Britain
Egyptian State Tourist Office Egyptian House. 170 Piccadilly. London W1V 9 DD, ENGLAND. (Tel 44171 493 5282, Fax: 44171 408 0295)

Canada
Egyptian Tourist Authority. 1253 McGill College Avenue, Suite #250. Montreal, Quebec H3B 2Y5. CANADA. (Tel: 514 861 4420, Fax: 514 861 8071)

France
Bureau du Tourisme Egyptien. Ambassade de la RAE. 90 Avenue des Champs Elysees. 75008. Paris, FRANCE. (Tel: 331 456 29442 / 456 29443, Fax: 331 428 93481)

Germany
Agyptishes Fremdenverkehrsamt, 64 A Kaiserstrasse, 60329 Frankfurt Main, GERMANY. (Tel: 4969 252 319, Fax: 4969 239 876)

Greece
Egyptian Tourist Authority. 5 Kolonaki St., Athens, 10671, GREECE. (Tel: 301 360 6906, Fax: 301 363 6681)

Italy
Egyptian Tourist Authority. Via Bissolati 19. 00187

Rome, ITALY. (Tel: 396 482 7985, Fax: 396 487 4156)

Japan
Egyptian Tourist Authority, Hoshinu Bldg. 3rd Floor 4 - 2. 2, Chome - Azabudai. Minatu - Ku. Tokyo, JAPAN. (Tel: 813 358 90653 / 358 90657, Fax: 813 358 91372)

Russia
Egyptian Tourist Authority, Trubnikovski. Pereulok 26, Apt 34. 131069 Moscow, RUSSIA. (Tel: 7095 290 2856, Fax: 7095 202 6158)

South Africa
Egyptian Tourist Authority. Regent Place Building (1st Floor). Mutual Gardens. Cradock Avenue. Rosebank, Johannesburg. P.O. Box 3298. SOUTH AFRICA. (Tel: 2711 880 9602, Fax: 2711 880 9604)

Spain
Oficina de Tourismo Egipto. Torre de Madrid. Planta 5, Oficina 3. Plaza de Espana. 28008 Madrid, SPAIN. (Tel: 341 559 2121, Fax: 341 547 5165)

Sweden
Egyptian Tourist Authority. Drottninggatan 65. S - 11136. Stockholm, SWEDEN. (Tel: 468 102 548, Fax: 468 102 541)

USA
Egyptian Tourist Authority. 645 North Michigan Ave., Suite #829, Chicago, IL 60611 USA (Tel: 312 280 4666 / 280 4693, Fax: 312 280 4788)
Egyptian Tourist Authority. 630 Fifth Avenue. Suite

#1706. New York, NY 10111, USA. (Tel 1212 332 2570, Fax: 1212 956 6439)

Egyptian Tourist Authority. 8383 Wilshire Boulevard. Suite #215. Beverly Hills, Los Angeles, CA 90211. USA. (Tel: 1213 653 8815, Fax: 1213 653 8961)

E.T.A. Offices in Egypt

Cairo *(Tel. Area Code: 02)*
Head Office, Adly St. (Tel: 391 3454)
Pyramids, near Hotel Mena House (Tel: 385 0259)
Cairo International Airport (Tel: 291 4255)
New Airport (Tel: 291 4277)
Railway Station (Tel: 764 214)

Alexandria *(Tel. Area Code: 03)*
Raml Station, Saad Zaghlul St. (Tel: 807 985)
Nuzha, Nuzha Airport (Tel: 425 8764)
Marine Passenger Station, Alex. Port (Tel: 492 5986)
Misr Railways Station (Tel: 492 5985, 803 494)

Port Said *(Tel. Area Code: 066)*
Main Office. Palestine St. (Tel: 223 868)
Reswah. Customs Area. (Tel: 21687-1)

Suez *(Tel. Area Code: 062)*
Main Office. Canal St. (Tel: 221 141)
Port Tawfeek (Town). Port Tawfeek. (Tel: 223 589)
Port Tawfeek (Port). (Tel: 32204)

Red Sea *(Tel. Area Code: 065)*
Hurghada. Bank Misr St. (Tel: 440 513)

El Minya *(Tel. Area Code: 086)*
Governorate Bldg. (Tel: 330 150)

Luxor *(Tel. Area Code: 095)*
Nile St. (Tel: 382 215)
Luxor Airport (Tel: 383 294)

Aswan *(Tel. Area Code: 097)*
Tourist Souk (Fair). (Tel: 323 297)

The New Valley *(Tel. Area Code: 088)*
El-Khargah. (Tel: 901 205)
Governorate Bldg. (Tel: 401 206)

Marsa Matruh *(Tel. Area Code: 03)*
Matruh. Governorate Bldg. (Tel: 394 3192)
Siwa. City Council Bldg. (Ext. 7)

North Sinai *(Tel. Area Code: 068)*
Al-Arish. Fouad Zikry St. (Tel: 341 016 / 340 4569)
Rafah. El Mena. (Tel: 300 655)

South Sinai *(Tel. Area Code: 068)*
Sharm El-Sheikh. (Tel: 768 385)

How to Get There

(Location Map on page 11)

By Air - Numerous airline companies fly into Cairo, and other major Egyptian cities. Egypt has several airports but only six are international ports of entry: Cairo, Alexandria, Luxor, Aswan, Hurghada (Ghardaka) and Sharm el Sheikh. Most air travellers enter Egypt through Cairo.

There are some cheap fares available, called 'bucket shops', which are basically tickets that have been distributed, by an airline, to selected travel agents. Airlines don't usually acknowledge/admit this practice. Check around with travel agencies.

Other ticket types include: Advance Purchase, Excursion Fares, Point-to-Point, ITX, Economy Class, Budget Fare, and Standby. Ask several people how much they paid, who sold them the tickets,...etc., to find the best deal for you.

As with any travel, it is best to pay by credit card, so you have the upper hand, in case you don't get a credible ticket.

By Land From Israel - Private vehicles are not permitted to enter Egypt from Israel; however, you may use public transportation and enter Egypt via Rafah on the northern coast of Sinai or from Eilat on the Red Sea. Buses run regularly from Tel Aviv and Jerusalem to the border at Rafah. At the border passengers leave from the Israeli vehicle, go through customs, and take an Egyptian bus or taxi.

If you are crossing from the town of Eilat, you will go through the Egyptian borderpost in Taba. From Taba there are buses and collective, or service taxis which go south to Nuweiba, Dahab and Sharm el Sheikh. A few of these buses also continue on to Cairo.

In Eilat, Israeli buses are permitted to enter Egypt and travel as far as Sharm el Sheikh at the southern tip of the Sinai.

If you plan to return to Israel, buy an open return ticket before you travel to Egypt.

By Land from Sudan or Libya - It is possible to enter Egypt from Sudan or Libya, but it is impractical.

By Boat from Europe - You may enter Egypt at Alexandria, or Port Said, along the Mediterranean Sea.

By Boat from the Sudan - There is a twice-weekly steamer that ferries cars the length of Lake Nasser, from Wadi Halfa in the Sudan to Aswan in Egypt. Information is available from the Nile Navigation Company Limited, Ramses Square (in the train station), and Nile Maritime Agency, 8 Quasr el Nil Street, both in Cairo; and the Nile Company for River Transport, 7 Atlas Building, Aswan. All arrangements to enter Sudan, including visas, must be made in Cairo. You must have a valid passport and either a transit or tourist visa to Sudan. If you plan to pass through Sudan you must have a valid visa for your next destination.

By Boat From Jordan or Saudi Arabia - A bus/ferry ticket is possible from Amman (Jordan) via Aqaba to Nuweiba in Sinai. The ferry runs twice a day between Aqaba and Nuweiba.

An Egyptian visa can be issued 'on the spot' at the Egyptian Consulate in Aqaba.

Where to Stay

Accomodation in Egypt ranges form cheap to expensive and rough to luxurious. There are hotels, pensions, youth hostels and a few camping grounds.

Hotels - Hotels are rated from one to five stars (luxury). The latter, live up to the expected luxury standards of international hotels, at very favourable prices. The rating system, for anything below the five-star class, seems inconsistent with Western standards. Hotels within a given class may vary widely in both price and quality of accommodation. Since conditions may change at any time, it is best to take the advice of a knowledgeable travel agent before booking. Since hotel prices will of course change along with the national and international economy, it seems pointless to include such information in this book.

Youth Hostels - Hostels are cheaper than the cheapest

hotels in Egypt. They are located in Cairo, Alexandria, Port Said, Aswan, Asyut, Damanhur, Marsa Matruh, Sohag, Suez, Sharm el Sheikh, and Hurghada. Prices vary, but all are nominal. Below, are the hostels in the Cairo area.

The Egyptian Youth Hostel Association office (Tel: 758099) at 7 Dr Abdel Hamid Street, Cairo, can give you the latest information.

El Manyal Youth Hostel - Abdel Aziz Street, Roda Island, Cairo. (Tel: 840729)

Kohinoor Youth Hostel - 8 Shoukri Street, off El-Ahram Street, Giza. (Tel: 852480).

Camping - Officially, camping is allowed at only a few places around Egypt. Even at the official sites, with a few exceptions, facilities tend to be basic. Outside the plots specifically set aside for camping, almost all the land is either desert or cultivated fields. Check around and get information and/or referrals, before using a site for camping.

What To Pack

• Sun protection is the single most important consideration for a trip to Egypt. Sunglasses, sunscreen, hat, and wind-chap screens are a must.

• A flashlight is important for exploring the interiors of monuments, and for nighttime exploring, as streetlights are sparse.

• A backpack or carry-all is practica,l to carry on your excursions. Pocket packages of tissues and/or a partial roll of toilet paper, tucked in your carry-all is useful.

• A money belt or pouch will give you some security for your money.

• Although most toiletries can be found in the major tourist areas, it is more convenient to bring your own contact lens

Planning Your Travel

solution, tampons, contraceptives, shampoo, etc.

• An insulated canteen is handy, but many tourists opt for the bottled water, tucked in their carry-all.

• Electric current is 220V AC, 50 Hz. Wall plugs are the round two-pronged European style. Electronic stores, such as Radio Shack, sometimes carry universal adaptors.

• Bring a supply of any medication you take regularly, and bring the prescription.

• Insect repellents (containing DEET), for mosquitoes and flies are important, especially in the summer, and in the delta area.

• It is always a good idea to travel with a small first-aid kit, filled with the standard items - Band-aids, antibiotic cream or ointment, an antiseptic agent, and an ointment to treat sunburn and itchy bites, etc.

• Medication for diarrhoea, such as Lomotil or Immodium, is recommended.

• Lens paper and cleaner and a dust brush are useful to keep your camera clean, with all the dust in Egypt.

• If you wear eyeglasses, carry a second pair or at least a copy of your prescription, in case of loss or breakage.

• Bring at least a few items of light, comfortable clothing to cope with early mornings or the winter cold snap. 100% cotton is preferable to synthetics, especially in the heat. Layers of light clothing are more practical than a single heavy item, since a clear winter day may start off cool but turn hot by midday. Also, it is usually cooler inside tombs and temples, than outside.

• Comfortable, sturdy shoes are essential; jogging shoes are better than boots.

• Bring one or two dressy outfits along, for evenings out and special occasions. At the Opera House, for example, a suit and tie are required.

• Most good hotels in Egypt have swimming pools. Bring a swimsuit and goggles, if you plan to swim.

Health & Vaccinations

Don't forget that you should always see your doctor for medical advice before leaving for a trip overseas.

Expect to do lots of walking, climbing, exposing yourself to the fine dust, plus the outdoor sun and wind. Stay fit.

Be sure you are caught up on all immunizations and vaccines before travelling. As with any international travel, it is best to contact the Center for Disease Control (http://www.cdc.gov), well in advance, for a current update on recommendations and precautions to take.

A vaccination certificate proving that you have been vaccinated for yellow fever and/or cholera is only necessary if you are coming from an infected area (such as most of sub-Saharan Africa and South America). These immunizations must be recorded in the International Certificate of Vaccination, the WHO card, issued by the World Health Organization. This document is obtained from authorized doctors in most countries. Persons without the proper immunizations are subject to a 36-hour quarantine at Cairo Airport.

If you are planning to visit the delta or other areas with a high concentration of mosquitoes, especially in the summer, a course of malaria treatment might be advisable, even though malaria is uncommon in Egypt.

Visas & Documents

A valid passport for at least six months from the date of arrival to Egypt and a visa are required. To obtain a visa please contact the nearest Egyptian Consulate:

USA
Washington (Tel: 202 232 5400, Fax: 202 332 7894)
New York (Tel: 212 759 7120, Fax: 212 308 7643)
Chicago (Tel: 312 443 1190, Fax: 312 443 1463)
San Francisco (Tel: 415 346 9700, Fax: 415 346 9480)

Houston (Tel: 713 961 4916, Fax: 713 961 3868)

Canada
Ottowa (Tel: 613 234 4931, Fax: 613 234 9347)
Montreal (Tel: 514 937 7781, Fax: 514 937 0588)

Processing of your visa application seems to vary according to nationality and where the application is made. Most people are given a three month tourist visa with either single or multiple entries. If you plan to return to Egypt after, for example, visiting Israel or Jordan, then you should request the multiple entry visa.

Tourists may be granted a one-month visa on arrival at Egyptian airports or ports. However, if you are coming from Israel, you can't get a visa at the border. You must get it at the Egyptian Consulate in Eilat or Tel Aviv, or elsewhere. There are no facilities for issuing visas at the Rafah border.

Student Discounts

Many places in Egypt offer handsome discounts for students. Obtain and carry your proof of student I.D. card with you everywhere. If you have an International Student Identification Card (ISIC), from the International Student Travel Confederation (http://www.istc.org), you can get discounts of 50% and sometimes more, on airfares, admission tickets to most places, ...etc. Always ask if a student discount is available.

Crime in Egypt

Egypt and its major cities, are almost crime-free zones. People may ask for money, but they will not steal it (except for a few cases of pickpockets), or harm you physically. If you can read Arabic, you will notice that the crime section of the Cairo newspaper is only about a quarter of a page.

4. Arriving & Departing

Visas at Point of Entry

If you wait until you get to the airport or port to obtain your visa, processing is usually quick and easy. A photograph is not required. At the airport, any of the numerous money exchange windows, which are located just before you get to the immigration/passport control booths, will sell you the necessary government stamps for the visa. When you exchange money at the bank booths, they will deduct the cost of the stamps from the total amount exchanged.

Airport Hustlers

Unfortunately, it is becoming more and more common at the airports (and elsewhere) of major cities throughout the world, that people will make a living taking advantage of tourists. You may be approached in the baggage claim area, at the airport, by a man or woman with an official-looking badge that says something like 'Egyptian Chamber of Tourism'. These people are not government tourism officials, they are trying to promote their hotels.

Customs

The visitor is permitted to enter Egypt with 250 grams of tobacco, or 50 cigars, one litre of alcohol, and personal effects.

Animals must have a veterinary certificate attesting to their good health, and a valid rabies certificate.

Cairo International Airport is one of the few airports that has a duty free shop upon arrival and departure.

Persons traveling with expensive electronic equipment such as cameras, video cameras, or computers, need to list these items in their passports to ensure that they will be exported upon departure.

Registration

You must register with the police within one week of your arrival in Egypt. Most hotels will take care of this, some for a small fee. It's worth having the hotel do it for you. The bigger hotels complete the registration formality without being asked to do so. Most package tourists don't even know it happens.

Antiquities Permits

Since some archaeological sites are not open to the general public for viewing, an antiquities permit is a useful thing to have, as it allows you easier access to many of these sites. To get the permit, from the Department of Antiquities in Abbassiya, Cairo, you might need a letter from the Archaeology Department of any university. Your tourist agent should advise you whether your choice of sites are open for public viewing, or if you will need the Antiquities Permit.

Travel Permits

Travel permits may be required for trips to certain parts of Egypt, such as westward past Marsa Matruh, for Siwa Oasis, and for some parts of the Nile Delta. Check with the main tourist office, at 5 Adly Street in Cairo, for the latest details.

Vaccinations

Vaccinations against cholera, yellow fever, tetanus, hepatitis, and a few other diseases are available in Cairo, at the Mogamma building, in Midan Tahrir. They will give you the standard yellow International Certificate of Vaccination card free. If you are getting a yellow fever vaccination, keep in mind that protection doesn't become effective until 10 days after vaccination.

Return Ticket

Most airlines require you to confirm your return ticket, at least 72 hours in advance of your departure. Make sure that you or your travel agency confirms your flight back home as soon as possible.

On Departure

Travellers are free to buy and export Egyptian goods, except items of antiquity - either ancient Egyptian or Islamic - including precious jewels, carpets, paintings or other works older than 100 years.

5. Getting Around in Egypt

What To Wear

Dress in layers of light clothing, which can be adjusted as the temperature changes throughout the day. The sun sets quickly, and when it does, the temperature drops significantly. There is a big difference in temperature inside tombs/temples, and the outdoors. It is worth repeating the caution to protect yourself against the bright Egyptian sun. For women, dress comfortably, but not sexily.

What to Carry With You

Your passport, always. A small bottle of water, pocket tissues and/or small roll of toilet paper, small medical kit, money - your larger bills in a safe place, and small bills and coins in a handy pocket for *baksheesh* (tips), as well as a torch/flashlight, hat, and mosquito repellent.

Calling Home

Local telephone calls can be made from public telephone booths, cigarette kiosks, major hotels and telephone offices. International calls can be made from the major hotels or telephone offices. Ask your hotel information desk..

Time

When it's 12 noon in Cairo it is; 10 am in London; 5 am in New York; and 7:30 pm in Sydney.

Newspapers & Magazines & Maps

• The *Egyptian Gazette* is Egypt's daily English-language newspaper.

• *Middle East Times* and *Al-Ahram Weekly* are two weekly English-language newspapers that offer coverage of regional and local news.

• The *Middle East Observer* is another weekly newspaper, but is geared more towards African and Middle Eastern readers.

• Other popular English-language magazines include: *Egypt Today, Business Today, Cairo Today,* and *Sports and Fitness*.

• Almost every major Western newspaper and news magazine can be found in Cairo, Alexandria, and other major tourist cities.

• You can get free maps from the offices of the Egyptian Tourist Authority.

Radio & Television

Egyptian radio and TV have several English-language programs. Check the *Egyptian Gazette* for the latest program information. You can also hear news from foreign sources, such as the BBC World Service and The Voice of America.

Several popular channels are aired in Egypt, including MNET, CNN, K-TV, MTV, and SuperSport, as well as some channels from Europe. A local TV station, Nile TV, offers programs in English and French. Channel 2 of the Egyptian TV, offers news in English and French.

Several American and British TV series appear on Egyptian TV. Most foreign programs are shown with Arabic subtitles.

Coping with the Environment

• Protect yourself against the heat of the sun in Egypt. Headaches, dizziness and nausea are signs of heat exhaustion. Drink plenty of fluids - don't wait until you are thirsty before drinking. Schedule your outdoor activities very early in the day, use sunscreen, wear a hat and sunglasses. Use a mild talcum powder to help avoid prickly heat, which is an itchy rash that strikes newcomers who haven't climatised yet.

• To avoid mosquito bites and the threat of malaria, use insect repellent, wear light-coloured clothing that covers most of your body, sleep near a fan, and use mosquito bednets at night.

Getting Sick in Egypt

• If anything serious happens, your hotel will be able to get a doctor for you. Your embassy can also provide assistance.

• Many travellers who stay in Egypt for more than a week are hit with Pharaoh's Revenge, which can combine upset stomach, diarrhoea, and possible slight fever. It is simply your system trying to adjust to a different environment. You are better off to be cautious, by experimenting slowly and gradually with the new (to you) delicious Egyptian food. If you encounter the revenge of the pharaoh, drink plenty of fluids (excluding milk, coffee, strong tea, soft drinks or cocoa), and stick with dried toast or maybe fresh yogurt.

Entocid, an antibiotic sold in most Egyptian pharmacies, can help.

If you are travelling, you may need to rely on medicine, such as Lomotil, Immodium, codeine phosphate tablets, a liquid derivative of opium prescribed by a doctor, or a medicine with pectin (like Kaopectate). Lomotil and/or Immodium are convenient because the pills are tiny. For children, Kaopectate is more advisable. If you are still ailing after all of this, see a doctor.

• There are hospitals throughout Egypt. Most of the doctors are well trained, with experience in a great variety of diseases and ailments. On the other hand, most medical facilities are not as well equipped as Western hospitals.

• There are a number of pharmacies in Cairo and other major cities, that operate 24 hours a day. Check with the information desk at any hotel.

Money Exchange & Credit Cards

The official currency of Egypt is called the pound (£E) or (EP). One Egyptian pound = 100 piastres. There are notes in denominations of 10, 25, and 50 piastres, as well as for 1, 5, 10, 20, 50 and 100 pounds. There are coins for 5, 10, and 25 piasters.

One U.S. dollar is usually worth EP 3.40.

The condition of the notes ranges from brand-new to totally-worn-out, so that you can barely discern the denomination.

Money can be officially changed at the airport, American Express offices, commercial banks, and most hotels. Most banks work evening hours for money exchange only.

Private exchange ofices are open most of the day and late into the evenings.

Save your receipts in case you have to change EP back into your currency when you leave.

Nile Activities

Feluccas are the ancient broadsail boats seen everywhere up and down the Nile. Taking a felucca ride while you're in Egypt is an absolute must; there's no better way to see the Nile, especially at sunset. If you don't have the time or inclination to spend several days on a felucca trip between sites of antiquities, you should at least try to hire one in Cairo, and take a leisurely cruise for a few hours. Sunset is one of the best times to take a felucca ride.

Feluccas congregate at several quays along the river, such as in Garden City, opposite the Meridien Hotel, or near Felfela in Maadi. The Maadi area has no bridges to obstruct the feluccas' path, so you get a longer trip with more variety of scenes/views. Mosquito repellent is vital in the marshy waters near Maadi.

The hourly price for feluccas now ranges from EP15 to EP20, depending on the size of the boat.

Casinos is the Egyptian term for outdoor restaurants along the Nile. They are open past midnight in the summer. They have very quiet and romantic settings. You may order food or beverages, usually at reasonable prices.

What To Eat

The Egyptian kitchen is renowned for its tasty dishes, which continue to grow in popularity, as word gets out. Elegant restaurants in major hotels, and elsewhere, offer delicious oriental selections such as Kofta, Kebab, Mulukhia, Tahina Salad, Baba Ghanough, Mixed Green Salad, Vine Leaves, Foul, Ta'meya and Kusheri.

The best food in Egypt is their fresh fruit and vegetables. As long as it has been washed, it is safe. A little moderation is advisable - it is easy to get carried away, and over-eat, when the food is so tasty and plentiful. Meat is safe as long as it has been thoroughly cooked. Avoid milk that hasn't at least been boiled, the same goes for cream. Milk in sealed cartons is safe to drink because it has been pasteurised and homogenised. Most processed and packaged ice cream is safe. Avoid anything raw, especially shellfish.

Egyptian restaurants often include a 12% service charge at the bottom of the bill. This money goes mostly towards the cost of purchasing and cleaning the staff uniforms. If you want to tip the waiter you have to add the baksheesh afterwards.

Places to Eat

There are thousands of cafes, teahouses and market stalls where you can find exotic or plain food and where it's easy to have a very filling meal for a few pounds. There are also plenty of restaurants serving international dishes and places where you can get Western fast food.

Breakfast
Almost all the major hotels offer all-you-can-eat breakfast buffets, included in the room prices. They usually offer an assortment of Egyptian and Western dishes.

Budget Eats - near Tahrir Square, Cairo
The Felfela Restaurant, near Midan el Tahrir, is a must, if you have the opportunity. The food is excellent, inexpensive, and the atmosphere is delightful.

Getting Around in Egypt

It's a good and a safe place to sample some popular Egyptian dishes.

Western Fast Food

There are several Wimpy bars in Cairo, for the British flavour. Pizza Huts, McDonald's, Arby's, and Kentucky Fried Chicken (KFC) are springing up all over the place. Other fast-food chains are arriving as well - too many to keep track of. They usually have clean, well-kept restrooms (a rarity in Egypt).

Floating Restaurants

Formal dinners and Nile dinner cruises can be enjoyed in several floating restaurants in Cairo. Ask the information desk of your hotel and/or your tour guide for suggested places and prices.

What To Drink

Tap water is generally safe to drink throughout Egypt, but drink it gradually rather than immediately. In the summer months, the tap water is heavily chlorinated, which makes the taste umpleasant.

Bottled mineral water is available everywhere, and easy to carry with you. Small local shops charge much less than the hotels.

Tea & Coffee

Tea and coffee are usually made quite strong. Tea is served in glasses at traditional Egyptian cafes, and in teacups at Western-style restaurants.

Specify clearly how much sugar you want beforehand, otherwise two or three big teaspoons of sugar may be automatically deposited into your glass. If you prefer unsweetened or lightly sweetened, just ask.

If you ask for coffee, you will probably get Turkish coffee, which is very strong. Drink it in small sips. As with tea, you have to specify how much sugar you want, unless you like it sweet.

If you want non-Turkish coffee, ask for "Nescafe". You will get a small packet of instant coffee, with a cup of hot water and cream.

Fruit Juices

On practically every street corner in every town throughout Egypt, there is a juice stand, where you can get a drink squeezed out of just about any fruit or vegetable you want. It is inexpensive, delicious, fresh, and very energizing. The sugarcane juice is tasty, very cheap, and something you may not find at home.

Other Non-Alcoholic Drinks

Soft drinks are very popular in Egypt and most major brands are available, including Coca-Cola, Sport Cola, Seven-Up, Fanta, Schweppes, and Pepsi. Diet soft drinks are becoming quite popular in Egypt, especialy Diet Coke, Pepsi and Seven-Up, but, as of this writing, they use saccarine, not Nutrasweet, so the taste may be different than what you are used to.

Remember that when it's hot, a soft drink will not quench your thirst. In fact, if anything, the sugar in it will dehydrate you more.

Alcohol

There are several alcoholic beverages available, that are produced in Egypt. The Egyptian beer is excellent, and is produced in two forms: Stella and Stella

Getting Around in Egypt

Export. Don't forget, beer was invented by ancient Egyptians! It is fun to sample the Egyptian wines too, which are pleasant.

For hard liquor, it's best to stick to the bars at major hotels rather than to small street bars. If you purchase a bottle from a store, make sure that the original seal is intact.

The Night Life

You shouldn't have any trouble finding nightclubs with floor shows, Western-style discos, and movie theatres with English-language movies, in Cairo, Alexandria, and other major cities. The major hotels also feature floor shows and/or discos. Many nightclubs can be found along Pyramids Road, in Giza.

Experience Egypt by walking along the Nile, Mingle with the people in the streets, or go to a casino along the Nile shore.

What To Read

Cairo, Alexandria, and other major cities, have several English language bookshops where you can find a satisfactory selection. However, the standard Western best-sellers, will be more expensive than back home, so bring along what you think you might need, if expenses are a concern.

A good selection of books about Egypt and the Egyptians, can be found at these same bookshops throughout Egypt, but a greater selection will be in Cairo and Alexandria. You will find books about people & society, fiction, history, languages, etc.

You can find a variety of maps in bookstores, tourist offices, and travel agencies.

What To Buy

Egypt is a great place to find inexpensive and elegant souvenirs.

• Papyrus artwork can be found everywhere, and is attractive and uniquely Egyptian.

• Hieroglyphic drawings of pharaohs, queens, and ***neteru*** (commonly known as *gods and goddesses*) can be found on an assortment of products.

• Brass plates engraved with various pharaonic scenes are well done and inexpensive.

• Similar scenes can also be found painted or appliqued onto cotton wall-hangings, or woven into small rugs.

• T-shirts and sweatshirts with Egyptian designs abound.

• Top quality Egyptian cotton is known to be the best in the world. Cotton shirts, pants, and gallabayas (the loose gowns worn by many Egyptian men and women) can be found at many shops. Gallabaya cloth can also be purchased by the metre (1.1 yd) to be made-to-order, or brought home as is. And don't forget the ever popular cotton T-shirts, in every colour and pattern imaginable.

• Gold (18k) and silver jewelry can also be made to specification for not much more than the cost of the metal. A cartouche with the name of a friend or relative spelled in hieroglyphics makes a great gift Be sure to order it early in your trip, so that it will be ready for pickup before you head back home.

• Another Egyptian specialty is the handblown Mouski glass, either blue or dark brown and filled with air bubbles. It is quite reasonable but very fragile. Don't worry - the merchants can pack it for you.

• Semiprecious stones, such as alexandrites, aquamarines, topaz, and turquoise are good buys and good memories of Egypt. Prices can be reasonable but it helps to know what you are purchasing.

Where to Go Shopping

The products in the hotel shops are pricey, but usually good quality, and might be convenient if you don't have much time, or don't care to shop.

You can get good prices at the bazaars, where there is lots of competition. It is a special Egyptian experience, to roam the narrow alleys of the bazaars, and find the souvenirs for all your friends back home. Enjoy the sights, smells, and sounds, and imagine that it was not much different, hundreds of years ago. Be prepared to bargain for everything - it is expected. Occasionally, drinks will be served, without obligation on your part to purchase anything. Enjoy yourself.

Communicating is easy. Most of the merchants know at least one foreign language. No matter what, they will find a way to communicate with you.

Khan el Khalili

Khan el Khalili is one of the largest bazaars in the Middle East, if not the world, and has been in existence for hundreds of years. It is located in the older part of (Islamic) Cairo. It is about 1,000 years old. It is a maze of alleyways and buildings, comprised of small shops, stalls, and workshops. If you ask for an item that is not on display, the merchant may excuse himself, disappear into a back alley, and return with whatever you requested. There is an air of competition and comradery.

Khan el Khalili bazaar is open from 10:00am to 9:00pm daily and closed Sunday.

Muski

Muski is a bazaar, similar to Khan el Khalili, but smaller and more frequented by the locals. Nothing should stop you from going there to look or to buy. Muski is located next to Khan el Khalili.

Souk al Attarin
Souk al Attarin is a spice bazaar, close to Khan el Khalili. This is a great experience for the senses, and worth a side-trip if time allows.

Harraniya & Kerdasa
These are two villages that manufacture tapestries. Harraniya is located on the canal road that takes you to Saqqara. Kardassa is off the Pyramid Road in Giza, on the way to the Pyramids.

Business Hours
Banks: 8:30am to 2:00pm daily, closed Friday, Saturday, and most holidays.

Business: 8:00am to 4-5pm, closed Friday, some on Saturday, and most holidays. Many grocery stores and gas stations are open 24 hrs a day, 7 days a week.

Government offices: 8:00am to 3pm daily, closed Friday and most holidays.

Shops: 10:00am to 9:00pm in winter, and 9:00am to 10:00pm in summer. Many shops are closed on Sunday.

Getting Around in Egypt

Transportation Between Cities

Egypt has a very expansive transportation system, both public and private. There are a wide variety of modes of travel, that can take you just about anyplace in Egypt.

Air

EgyptAir (Tel: 390 2444, 372 444) flies from Cairo to Alexandria, Marsa Matruh, Luxor, Aswan, Abu Simbel, El-Wadi el Gadded (New Valley) at Kharga Oasis (twice a week), Hurghada, and Taba.

Sinai Air (Tel: 760 948, 776 894) flies from Cairo to Hurghada, Al Arish, Taba, Sharm el Sheikh, St. Catherine's Monastery, El Tor, and Tel Aviv, Israel.

In Egypt, air fares are about average, by international standards.

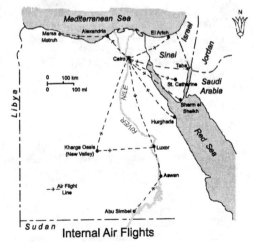

Internal Air Flights

Train

• The Egyptian State Railway is a government-owned system founded in 1851, which services the entire Nile Valley south to Aswan, the Suez Canal cities of Suez, Ismaillia, and Port Said, the Delta cities, and Northern Coast cities of Alexandria and Marsa Matruh. Sleeper compartments with meals included, are available.

There are at least half a dozen through trains a day on major routes. Fares are inexpensive, but unless one is traveling with a tour, tickets must be purchased at the main railway stations (in Cairo at the Ramses Station at Midan Ramses), or a few select major subway stations. Use your International Student Identification Card (ISIC) for discounts.

• There is one privately-owned train operating in Egypt, namely the Wagon Lits sleeper, with first, second, and third class compartments. The cars are similar to the ones used in Europe. They run Cairo-Luxor-Aswan, and back. The express trains travel overnight from Cairo to Luxor to Aswan and back again, leaving Cairo at around 7 in the evening, and arriving in Aswan at 9 the following morning. Bookings are one week in advance through a travel agent or from:

Compagnie Internationale des Wagons Lits Egypte
 9 Menes Street, Heliopolis, Cairo (Tel: 290 8802/4)
 48 Giza Street, Giza (Tel: 348 7354, 349 2365)

• Regular night trains with sleeper compartments and meals included, leave every day, and cost much less than the Wagon Lits fares. Reservations must be made in advance.

Getting Around in Egypt

Egypt Railways

Bus

A network of deluxe air-conditioned, comfortable buses travel to almost all the main towns of Egypt. Get the latest information from your nearest tourist office or hotel, about location of terminals and schedule of buses. Beware, the volume level of the Arabic videos shown on the buses is usually quite high. Bring along earplugs if you are hoping to sleep.

The following is a list of the major bus offices in Cairo:
Middle Delta Bus Co. (Tel: 946 286, 946 752)
East Delta Bus Co. (Tel: 261 1882)
International Service Station (Sinai) (Tel: 839589, 824753, 743027, 260 9307 Nasr City)
Upper Egypt Bus Co. (Tel: 746 658), Qolali
West Delta Bus Co. (Tel: 759 701 Tahrir, 760 422 Ahmed Helmy).

Taxi (Between Cities)

These types of co-op taxis (called *service taxis* by the locals), congregate near bus and train stations. The taxi driver will wait until a group of six or seven passengers fill the taxi, and then will begin the trip. Cost sharing makes the prices reasonable.

Boat

Feluccas, the ancient sailboats of the Nile, are still the most common means of transport up and down the river. The best trip to make, is the journey between Aswan and Esna, Edfu or Kom Ombo, which can take from one to three days.

Nile Cruises

This is a beautiful, relaxing, memorable way to visit the sites of antiquity in Egypt. The most practical cruise for most people, is a 3-5 day tour, between Luxor and Aswan. You can relax on the deck of the ship, and enjoy the lush, green, scenery along the shores, as you slowly make you way up/down the Nile. The ship stops at various times along the way, to allow you to visit the sites in that area. They usually stop at Edfu, Esna, and Kom Ombo.

Longer cruises are available too, for as long as three weeks, that begin/end at Cairo.

You have the opportunity to meet and get to know a group of people from all over the world, as you all share the excursions and discussions along the way, in a pleasant atmosphere.

A variety of sizes of ships and prices are available. Your travel agent can provide a selection to meet your needs. If you are travelling in the warmer months of the year, make sure the ship provides air-conditioning.

Driving/Rental Cars

Once you are in Cairo, you may decide to leave the driving to others. If you want to drive, it is recommended that you have experience in Cairo driving, and to make sure that you have an international driving license.

Driving in Sinai is a different story - the traffic is light, and the roads spacious. It would be great to have a car, or better still, a 4-wheel-drive vehicle.

The following car rental agencies have offices in Cairo:
- *Avis* - 16, Ma'mal al-Sukar St. Garden City (Tel: 354 7081).
- *Hertz* - 195, 26 July St., Agouza (Tel: 347 4172).
- *Budget* - 1, Mohamed Ebeid-St., Heliopolis (Tel: 291 8244).
- *Bita* - 15, Mahmoud Basyuni St. (Tel: 746 169).
- *Max Rent-a-Car*, 27 Lebnan Street, Mohandeseen. (Tel: 347 4712/3, Fax: 341 7123). There is a branch office in Sharm el Sheikh, for four-wheel drive vehicles, with or without experienced desert drivers.

Sunshine Tours & Services, 106 Muhammad Farid St. (Tel: 760 559, 393 1955).

The roads from Cairo to Upper Egypt are the longest, most congested, and most dangerous in Egypt. It is not advisable to drive at night, as there are many additional hazards, such as vehicles that stop completely with lights out, donkey carts which move along slowly with no lights, and taxis and overloaded trucks that travel too fast and recklessly.

There are petrol (fuel) stations throughout the country, with those operated by Mobil, Esso, Shell, and Egyptian oil companies offering many 24-hour service with mini-markets on the premises. Fuel, inexpensive and sold by the litre, is available in 90 octane which is super, or 80, which is regular. 90 is better for most purposes.

Road signs are similar to those used throughout Europe. Driving is on the right-hand side of the road. Speed limits are posted on major highways and are enforced by radar. When you wish to pass, sound your horn very deliberately, in order to make it clear that you are going to do something extraordinary. Egyptian drivers need an extra signal, since nearly all of them over-use the horn, even when nobody is around. Another bad habit is blinking the high beam at night. When a car is approaching, he may blind you. Blink back, and he may stop. He may be checking to see if you are awake.

Distances between Cairo and other cities:

City	Kilometers	Miles
Alexandria (Delta Road)	225	140
Alexandria (Desert Rd)	221	138
Damietta	191	119
Barrages	25	15

Minya	236	151
Asyut	359	224
Luxor	664	415
Esna	719	449
Edfu	775	484
Kom Ombo	835	521
Aswan	880	550
Port Said	220	137
Ismaillia	140	87
El Fayoum Oasis	103	64
Bahariya Oasis	316	197
Farafra Oasis	420	262
Dakhla Oasis	690	413
Kharga Oasis	586	366

Transportation Within Cities

Bus
Cairo and Alexandria are the only cities in Egypt with their own bus systems. They vary in size (mini/micro/regular) and price, but are always very cheap.

Tourist Buses
Tourist buses are costly, but quite comfortable. Their destinations are limited to the major tourist attractions, but the drivers may make a few stops along the way, at shops and restaurants of the drivers' relatives and friends.

Metro/Subway
Cairo is the only city in Egypt with a metro/subway system. Cairo now has two lines, with 40 stations that stretch for 60 km (37 mi) from the southern suburb of Helwan to El

Marg near Heliopolis, and from downtown to Shubra. The metro is fast, clean, inexpensive and usually not crowded. More and more subway lines are being constructed.

Tram

Cairo and Alexandria are also the only two cities with tram systems. Alexandria's trams are relatively efficient and go all over the city but they also get quite crowded. Cairo's trams are gradually being phased out. The trams are as cheap as, and sometimes cheaper than, the buses.

Taxi (Local)

Most cities in Egypt have local taxis. There are two kinds of taxi, metered and unmetered. Whichever type of taxi you choose, if you're uncertain about the fare, then first consult a local for the going rate, then negotiate the price before you get in.

The best method for paying is to get out of the cab when you arrive at your destination, stick the money through the front passenger's side window and walk away. If the driver objects, and the negotiation reaches a high volume, then mention the police. The driver will then either accept your price, or agree to see the police, in which case, he is bluffing, or your fare really is too low.

For longer trips, such as to the airport or pyramids, the driver will usually insist on setting the price.

It's quite common to share a taxi with other passengers.

Waterbus

Two waterbus lines carry passengers along the Nile. The first line begins in the front of the big, round Radio & Television building and goes north as far as the Nile barrages and Qanater, at the tip of the Nile Delta. The other waterbus line goes south and stops near Cairo University, Old Cairo and Maadi. The fare is set and nominal.

Limousine Services

Limousines are available for those who want to travel in style and privacy. You do have to know where you want to go, and to make sure the driver knows as well. Unless you are able to resist very politely, you will also be subjected to visits at shops and/or restaurants of his relatives and friends.

The following services are available, in Cairo:

Bita Limousine Service, Gazirah Sheraton. (Tel: 341 1333 / 341 1555). Marriott Hotel (Tel: 340 8888).

Budget Limousine Service, Semiramis Intercontinental Hotel (Tel: 355 7171 x 8991).

Limousine Misr, 7 Aziz Bil-Lah, Zeitoun. (Tel: 259 9813/4).

Egyptrav, Nile Hilton. (Tel: 755 029, 766 548, 393 2644).

Bicycle

Bicycles are a practical way of getting around smaller towns and their surrounding sites. In most places, particularly Luxor, you can rent a bicycle quite cheaply. Bicycles are, however, somewhat impractical for travelling long distances.

Walking

This works great for short distances, or combined with another method. If you can see the Nile from where you are, walk there, and enjoy a real flavour of Egypt.

Hiking as a pastime is not popular in Egypt, and should not be undertaken in remote areas without a local guide. That said, there are interesting hikes, and local people may be willing to act as guides in the Eastern Desert, Sinai and the Oases.

Hitchiking is not a common practice in Egypt and is not recommended, especially for women.

6. Historical Information

Below, is a rough summary of the main periods of Egypt's history:

Pre-Dynastic Pharaonic Egypt (?? - 3200 BCE)
Dynastic Pharaonic Times   (3200-343 BCE)
Greek Rule   (332 - 30 BCE)
Roman & Byzantine Rule   (30 BCE - 640 CE)
The Arab Rule   (640 - 1517)
Turkish Rule   (1517 - 1882)
British Occupation   (1882 - 1956)
Independent Egypt   (1952 onwards)

BCE denotes Before Common Era, also noted in other references as B.C.
CE denotes Common Era, also noted in other references as A.D.

Pre-Dynastic Era (?? - 3200 BCE)

How old is Egypt, you might ask?

• The Greek and Roman writers of antiquity, basing their accounts on information received either first or second-hand from Egyptian sources, claimed a far greater antiquity for the Egyptian civilization than that currently established by Academic Egyptologists. These Egyptian sources called for antiquity ranging from 24,000 and 36,000 years during which Egypt was civilized.

• Herodotus reported that he was informed by Egyptian priests that the sun had twice set where it now rose, and twice risen where it now set. Egyptologist Schwaller de Lubicz explained the statement to mean that it may be a reference to the progressional cycles of the equinox. The progression results in the rising against a different sign of the Zodiac approximately every two thousand years. This would mean that the Egyptians counted their history back for at least a cycle and a half, some 36,000 years. This is in a general agreement with other accounts and evidential findings throughout Egypt.

• Even though the above reports were current in those Late Kingdom and Ptolemaic days, most Academic Egyptologists continue ignoring them because they lack physical evidence to support an antiquity of this order. Since such remote antiquity is hard to handle, they ascribe these legendary millennia to the Egyptian imagination. It is, however, difficult to provide convincing archaeological evidence that is older than 5,000 to 7,000 years or longer, because nothing of meaningful value can logically survive such a long time. Circumstantial evidence, from varied historical sources, can be as strong or even stronger than physical archaeological evidence. As such, we should continue to mention the different sources of information, and not to arbitrarily choose to ignore or accept them.

• The Greco-Egyptian historian Manetho (3rd century BCE), under the early Ptolemies, wrote the only substantive history of Egypt to come down to us. He gathered his information from Egyptian records. A few pre-dynastic inscribed tablets and papyri have been found, but all were incomplete because of their remote age. Manetho acknowledged greater antiquity of the Egyptian history. However, because of the overwhelming task, he chose **Mena**(*Menes*) as a starting point, about 3000 years earlier.

The Glorious Pharaonic Era
[Dynastic Egypt] (3200-343 BCE)

Manetho started with ***Mena****(Menes)* and then divided the entire chronicle of events into thirty-one dynasties, from ***Mena****(Menes)* to the conquest of Alexander the Great in 332 BCE. Manetho's list of kings and their years of rule have been preserved in the writings of early Christian record keepers. Modern historians selectively use such records, and accept the numbering of Manetho's dynasties, which seems to follow very ancient practice. They also continue to use the Greek versions of the pharaohs' and ancient sites' names.

We, however, in this book, will use the legitimate Egyptian names in ***bold italics***. In order not to burden the readers, other names given arbitrarily and disrespectfully by the Greeks and Arabs, will be shown in *regular italics*.

The thirty-one Dynasties of Manetho, have been further grouped by modern historians into larger time-spans, so as to coincide with distinct cultural patterns, separated by unknown periods of political uncertainties. Sometimes these periods are further sub-divided.

Estimated dates for the dynasties are given below. Those before the Twenty-Sixth Dynasty are approximations. The dates of individual kings, queens and other individuals mentioned in the book will be found throughout the book, in conjunction with each subject.

Neolithic Period - before 5000 BCE
Pre-Dynastic Period - c. 5000-3300 BCE
Proto-Dynastic Period - c. 3300-3050 BCE

Historical Information

Dynasty	Dates	
I	3050 BCE - 2890 BCE	Early
II	2890 BCE - 2649 BCE	Dynastic
III	2649 BCE - 2575 BCE	Period
IV	2575 BCE - 2465 BCE	
V	2465 BCE - 2323 BCE	Old
VI	2323 BCE - 2150 BCE	Kingdom
VII-X - 1st Interm. Period	2150 BCE - 2040 BCE	
XI	2040 BCE - 1991 BCE	Middle
XII	1991 BCE - 1783 BCE	Kingdom
XIII-XVII - 2nd Interm. Period	1783 BCE - 1550 BCE	
XVIII	1550 BCE - 1307 BCE	New
XIX	1307 BCE - 1196 BCE	Kingdom
XX	1196 BCE - 1070 BCE	
XXI (Tanis)	1070 BCE - 712 BCE	Third
XXII (Libyan)	945 BCE - 712 BCE	Interm.
XXIII (Nubia&Thebes)	878 BCE - 712 BCE	Period
XXIV (Sais)	740 BCE - 712 BCE	
XXV (Nubia &Thebes)	712 BCE - 657 BCE	
XXVI (Sais)	657 BCE - 525 BCE	
XXVII (Persian)	525 BCE - 404 BCE	Late
XXVIII (Sais)	404 BCE - 399 BCE	Kingdom
XXIX	399 BCE - 380 BCE	
XXX	380 BCE - 343 BCE	
Second Persian Period	343 BCE - 332 BCE	
Macedonian Kings	332 BCE - 304 BCE	Greco-
Ptolemic Dynasty	323 BCE - 30 BCE	Roman
Roman Emperors	30 BCE - 323 CE	Period
Byzantine Emperors	323 CE - 640 CE	

Ptolemaic Era (332-30 BCE)

Alexander the Great entered Egypt unopposed. He was even welcomed by the Egyptians, who wanted help getting rid of the Persian occupiers, at any cost. He founded the city of Alexandria. After his death, the Ptolemaic Dynasty was founded, and Alexandria flourished. Disputes and Ptolemies' in-fighting ended their rule, about the time of Cleopatra's suicide. Afterwards, Egypt became a Roman Province.

Roman & Byzantine Rule (30 BCE -640 CE)

Egypt became a Roman colony, and was made the granary of the Roman Empire. The Romans succeeded in protecting the Egyptian borders.

Shortly after Christianity was declared the state religion, in the 4th century, the Roman Empire split in half. The eastern half became what was later known as the Byzantine or Eastern Empire. It was ruled from Constantinople (now Istanbul), while the Western Roman Empire remained centred in Rome.

The Byzantines continued to successfully protect the Egyptian borders, until 640 CE, when the Arabs arrived.

Arab Rule (640-1517)

The Arabs entered Egypt, in 640 CE, and made Egypt an Arab colony with Islam as its religion, and Arabic as its language. This was the devastating blow to ancient Egypt.

In 658 CE, the Omayyads, an Arab dynasty based in Damascus, snatched control of Egypt and stayed in power until 750 CE. For the next 108 years Egypt was ruled by the Baghdad-based Abbasid Dynasty.

Arabic Islamic dynasties then made Cairo their capital city, and kept changing hands, killing each other, to take over power, until the Turkish soldiers arrived.

Turkish Rule (1517-1882)

In 1517, Egypt was invaded by Ottoman sultans, who relied on Mamelouks (slaves) to govern the country.

In 1798, Napoleon conquered Egypt, but left three years later.

An Albanian officer in the Ottoman service, called Mohamed Ali, declared himself ruler of the Egypt. During his reign (1805-1849), Egypt made progressive changes. However, under the rule of his grandson, Khedive Ismail, his financial mis-management led to the British invasion of Egypt, in 1882 CE.

British Occupation (1882-1956)

The British maintained their forces throughout the whole country. But gradually, their military forces shrank from populated areas, to station near the Suez Canal, until a total withdrawel treaty was signed, and all the British forces left Egypt, in 1956.

Independent Egypt

In 1952, the royal dynasty established by Mohamed Ali came to an end when a group of army officers forced the abdication of King Farouk. It was the first time in about 2,000 years, that Egyptians finally ruled themselves - not as in the Pharaonic time, but under the domination of Arabic/Islamic traditions.

In 1954, Egypt was proclaimed a republic, and Gamel Abdel-Nasser became her president. After his death in 1970, Nasser was succeeded by Mohamed Anwar El-Sadat, who was assassinated in 1981. Mohamed Hosni Moubarak was elected to Presidency, at this time, and was re-elected when his seven year term expired.

7. Understanding Ancient Egyptians

The general image of Egypt is that of the pyramids, sphinx, temples, and a rather nasty pharaoh. This nasty fellow probably had a whip and was forcing those poor enslaved Israelites to build large structures to satisfy his ego. Such an image has more to say about Cecile B De Mille's Hollywood extravaganzas than history. The sad thing is that a large amount of our 'Egyptology' has been molded by Judeo-Christian anti-Egyptian prejudice. Even if we consider we are in a 'post-Christian' culture, these images still have more of an effect than we ever would like to admit. The 19th century paradigm of Egyptology continues until this day, even though it now possesses a veneer of scholarship and scientific investigation.

Religion

To understand the ancient Egyptians, is to understand their 'religion' (for lack of a better term).

The Egyptians regarded the universe as a conscious act of creation by the One Great God. The fundamental doctrine was the unity of the Deity. <u>This One God was never represented</u>. It is the functions and attributes of his domain that were represented. Once a reference was made to his functions/attributes, he became a distinguishable agent; reflecting this particular function/attribute, and its influence on the world. His various functions and attributes as the Creator, Healer, and the like, were called the *neteru* (singular: *neter* in the masculine form and *netert* in the feminine form). As such, an Egyptian *neter/netert* was not a *god/goddess* but the personification of a function/attribute of the One God.

Central to their complete understanding of the universe, was the knowledge that man was made in the image of God, and as such, man represented the created image of all creation. Accordingly, Egyptian symbolism and all measures were therefore simultaneously scaled to man, to the earth, to the solar system, and ultimately to the universe.

The Egyptian thinking that the One God can be represented through his functions/attributes is reflected in mankind. Each one of us has various functions and attributes. A person can be a teacher in the classroom, a father to his children, a husband to his wife, a player on his team, ... etc. This person does not have multiple personalities, but multiple functions/attributes.

Egyptians recognized the universal validity of this kind of thinking, and applied it to all the levels of the hierarchically organized world. Even though it may appear complex at first sight, it is both coherent and consistent with experience. This was the essence of the Egyptian philosophy. It is a real philosophy based on organized, systematic, consistent and coherent principles.

The totality of the Egyptian civilization was built upon a complete and precise understanding of universal laws, in all aspects of life.

For the people of Egypt, there were no perceived differences between sacred and mundane actions, as we moderns believe there to be. Every action, no matter how mundane: plowing, sowing, reaping, brewing, building ships, etc. - was viewed as an earthly symbol for a specific divine activity.

The cosmological ideas of ancient Egypt were expressed by myth and symbolism, which are a superior means for expressing metaphysical concepts, and achieving understanding of complex issues. Abstract information is useless, unless it is transformed into understanding of these concepts.

It is important to realize that for Egyptians, every *physical* fact of life had a *symbolic* meaning. At the same time, every *symbolic* act of expression had a *material* background.

The typical Egyptian tomb sowing and reaping scene parallels the biblical parable "Whatsoever a man soweth, that shall he also reap".

This was intended to be a spiritual message, not agricultural advice.

The Neteru(gods/goddesses)

The *neteru*(*gods*) were the personification of the energies/powers/forces that, through their actions and interactions, the universe was created, maintained, and continues to be maintained.

In order to simplify and convey the scientific and philosophical abstracts of the *neteru*(*gods*), some fixed representations were invented. As a result, the figures of **Ptah**, **Ausar**(*Osiris*), **Amen**, **Heru**(*Horus*), **Mut**, etc., became the signs of such attributes/functions/forces/energies.

The figures of the *neteru* were intended merely to fix the attention or to represent abstract idea(s), and were not intended to be looked upon as real personages.

Animal Worship

Egyptians' cosmic consciousness and careful observation of the natural world, revealed to them that certain animals had specific qualities that could symbolize certain divine functions and principles, in a particularly pure and striking fashion. As such, certain animals were chosen as symbols for that particular aspect of divinity.

There was no animal worship in ancient Egypt. The animal-headed *neteru*(*gods*) were symbolic expressions of a deep spiritual understanding of the universe. This view is also shared by the Hermetic orders, Masonic orders, and the Renaissance Neoplatonists.

Symbolism & Neteru (Egyptian Caricature)

Egyptian symbolism could be compared in some sense to modern day caricature. Caricature uses symbols, (such as Uncle Sam, Russian bear, British bulldog, etc.), to represent concepts, ideas, nations, ...etc. A symbol reveals to the mind a reality other than itself. For the informed, the cartoon can reveal, in legitimate symbolic form, the totality of a given situation, in the eyes of the individual cartoonist. For those unfamiliar with the cartoonist and his/her choice of symbols, the cartoon will be total nonsense.

In Egyptian symbolism, the precise role of the *neteru* (*gods*) was revealed in many ways: by dress, headdress, crowns, feathers, animal, plant, colour, position, size, gesture, sacred object, or type of symbolic equipment (e.g., flail, scepter, staff, ankh). Only those initiated into symbolic language, can contemplate a wealth of physical, physiological, psychological and spiritual data, in all the symbols.

☞ Without recognizing the simple fact about the intent of symbolism, we will continue to be ignorant of the wealth of Egyptian knowledge and wisdom.

Their Language

Our main access to the ancient Egyptian history is restricted by our knowledge of their language. The Rosetta stone (found in 1799) is our only key to read and understand hieroglyphics. The stone consists of fourteen partial lines of Egyptian hieroglyphics, thirty-two lines of Egyptian Demotic (a cursive type script), and fifty-four lines of ancient Greek.

Champollion was able to match the hieroglyphs to the Greek, by comparing two cartouches on the tablet, containing glyphs that read *Ptolemaios* and *Cleopatra*. These two names became the keys to deciphering the hieroglyphics.

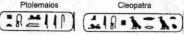

Champollion followed up his discovery of the two names by intense study. By 1822, he was able to decipher names, inscriptions and short sentences.

From the few words on the Rosetta stone, Champollion and other Egyptologists began to learn more about the hieroglyph symbols and the rules of grammar.

The discovery of the Rosetta Stone revived the ancient language, which was forbidden to be used since the seventh century, when Egypt became an Arab colony.

As in all Semitic styles of writings, hieroglyphic writing was limited to the consonants of the words, because the meaning of the word was generally contained in the consonants, while the vowels were added only to indicate the grammatical forms. As such, vowel sounds were not included in the written language.

Since we do not know the exact sounds of their words, and to simplify matters, academic Egyptologists used the sounds of some Coptic words (basically ancient Egyptian words written in the Greek alphabet) to estimate the sounds of the unwritten ancient Egyptian vowels.

Therefore, the vowels you see in translated Egyptian texts are an approximation, and by no means do they represent the true sound.

As a result, you may find a variety in writing the same thing such as Atam/Atum/Atem/Atom. The *A* at the beginning of the word is not considered a vowel by the ancients, but rather a consonant (the letters *aleph* and *ayin*).

The hieroglyphic form of writing, like many things in ancient Egypt, was the  result of profound knowledge of a cosmic nature.

The image of each Egyptian symbol contained a specific cosmic meaning. This meaning was also amplified by the sound of the letter itself. Words were constructed of these letters in a manner incorporating and amplifying the meaning of the individual symbols, so that the meaning of a word emerged from the interplay of these symbols.

The ancient Egyptian language was a picture of reality.

The word was very powerful because the word was an image. Every picture was potentially animate. A common expression, in our times, is that a picture is worth a thousand words. The same applies to the pictorial hieroglyphs, which not only had an overt phonetic script, but a more hermetic symbolism, which conveyed the subtler metaphysical realities of the universe. As such, it evoked an idea or concept in its entirety.

Below, are the commonly estimated Latin letters that are equivalent to the hieroglyphic symbols, as estimated by academic Egyptologists:

A	A	B	CH	CH	CH	D	F
G	H	H	I	J	K	M	N
P	Q	R	S	SH	T	W	Y

Egypt also had a kind of shorthand system of hieroglyphs called *hieratic*, which was used for official communications and other secular matters.

A still more cursive script, *demotic* was employed, presumably used for economic concerns.

The Per-aa(*Pharaoh*)

The Egyptian word for *Pharaoh* is ***Per-aa***, meaning *The Big House*, in a loving and caring sense. The ***per-aa***(*pharaoh*) was a representative of the people in a far more profound sense than that implied by the modern use of the phrase. His function was fundamentally religious. When a pharaoh states, "I did so and so" that *'I'* was, in the spiritual sense, quite objective and impersonal. His declaration is not different than when Christ declared in the Gospels, "I am the way, the truth and the life."

Despite the repeated charges of vanity against the pharaohs, it is worth remembering that they lived in homes of mud-brick, the same material used by the humblest peasants.

One of the principal ceremonies connected with the coronation was the anointing of the king, and his receiving the emblems of majesty from the ***neteru***. The king was not anointed with oil, but with the fat of the crocodile. MeSSeH was the word for crocodile, in ancient Egypt. The word *Messiah*, meaning *Anointed*, originated from MeSSeh, the ancient Egyptian word signifying the ritual of anointing the king.

The pharaoh's conduct and mode of life were regulated by prescribed rules. Laws were laid down in the sacred books, for the order and nature of his occupations. He was forbidden to commit excesses; even the kind and quality of his food were prescribed with precision. He was constantly reminded of his duties, both in public and in private.

War had a profound religious significance in ancient Egypt. It symbolized the forces of order controlling chaos and the light triumphing over darkness.

The typical scene on the outer walls of Egyptians temples, shows the King, the royal principle, controlling the power of darkness in order to ensure the order in the temple.

The famous war scenes of Ramses II, at Kadesh, are a good example of the concept of war in ancient Egypt. Ramses is shown both betrayed and abandoned by his own troops. This theme of betrayal and abandonment also occurs in other military friezes by other kings, which is a strong indication that we are dealing with symbolism, not a historical event. The "enemy" is always the power of darkness and chaos. The king is the spiritual principle. Betrayal and abandonment result from reliance on earthly supports.

Sacred Texts - Their Writings

Most Egyptian funerary and religious writings derive from the earlier Unas Funerary (commonly known as *Pyramid*) Texts. These compositions are known as: <u>The Book of the Coming Forth by Day</u> (commonly known as <u>The Book of the Dead</u>), <u>The Book of What Is In the Duat</u> (or Underworld), <u>The Book of the Gates</u>, <u>The Book of Caverns</u>, <u>The Litany of Ra</u>, <u>The Book of Aker</u>, <u>The Book of Day</u> and <u>The Book of Night</u>. Each of these texts emphasizes specific aspects of the Egyptian understanding of the cycle of life/death/rebirth. <u>The Book of the Caverns</u> has a psychological focus; and its theme of punishment and reward is paramount. <u>The Book of the Gates</u> has a spiritual focus. <u>The Book of What Is In the Duat</u> has a magical/alchemical focus. <u>The Book of Day</u> and <u>The Book of Night</u> highlight cosmological and astronomical aspects.

<u>The Book of the Coming Forth by Day</u>, wrongly translated and commonly known as <u>The Egyptian Book of the Dead</u>, consists of over a hundred chapters of varying lengths, which were mostly derived from the Unas funerary texts (commonly known as Pyramid Texts). This book is to be found, in its complete form, only on papyrus scrolls that were wrapped in the mummy swathings of the deceased and buried with him.

Temples

An Egyptian temple was not a place of public worship. It was the study centre and shrine for the ***neter***(*god*), who represented some specific aspect of the One God. Only the priesthood had access to the inner sanctuaries, where the sacred rites and ceremonies were performed. In some instances, only the King himself or his authorized substitute had permission to enter.

The choice of location and design peculiarities of a temple were not based on economical considerations, but rather on a deeper knowledge, of which we are still unaware.

Great temples were not built quickly, or by one king alone. Such temples were built over the years, by successive kings.

In general, the Egyptian temple was surrounded by a massive wall of mud-brick. This wall isolated the temple from its surroundings which, symbolically, represented the forces of chaos. Metaphorically, the mud resulted from the union of heaven and earth. The brick wall itself was therefore set in wavy courses to symbolize the primeval waters, representing the first stage of creation.

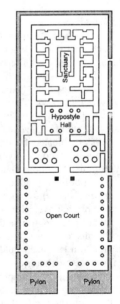

The exterior walls of the temple resembled a fortress, so as to defend it against all forms of evil. The temple was entered through two pylons, beyond which lay an open court. This court sometimes had colonnades along the sides and an altar in the middle. Next, along the temple-axis, came the hypostyle, a pillared hall often surrounded by small rooms which are used for the storage of temple equipment and for other secondary functions. Finally, there was the sanctuary, which was a dark room containing the shrine, where the figure of the *neter* was placed. The sanctuary was called the *Great Seat*. The sanctuary's doors were shut and sealed all year long, and were open only for the great festivals. Outside the walls of the temple were the residences of the priestly staff, the workshops, storerooms, and other ancillary structures.

The Obelisks

Temples had obelisks placed at their entrances.

Each obelisk was made of a single piece of pink granite. Like all the pink granite of Egypt, it was quarried several hundred miles to the south, at *Sunt*(*Aswan*), transported several miles to the Nile, loaded onto a cargo ship, floated down to *Ta-Apet*(*Thebes*), where it was unloaded, transported on land, and then set up on its pedestal with perfect accuracy.

Ritual reliefs show the pharaoh single-handedly raising an obelisk by means of a single rope, tied to its upper extremity. This is of course symbolic. According to the famed Egyptologist Franqois Daumas, the erection of the obelisk was a symbolic reproduction of the Tet pillar, the familiar *Ausarian*(*Osirian*) symbol standing for the backbone (i.e., support) of the physical world and the channel through which the divine spirit might rise through matter to rejoin its source.

The shadows cast by the pair of unequal obelisks, at the entrance to a temple, would enable the astronomer/priests to obtain precise calendrical and astronomical data, relevant to this given location. Egyptians were then able to coordinate such data with similar readings from other key sites which are also furnished with their peculiar obelisks.

Monument Usurping

Egyptian pharaohs have been unjustly accused of appropriating each others' works. In some cases, a later king had removed the name of the earlier king responsible for the original building, and replaced it with in his own. Some pharaohs re-used stones, or built on top of an existing temple. Some conclude then, that the later king willfully "appropriated" the work of the earlier. Yet, these "appropriations" are selective and not arbitrary. Only certain names in certain places have been removed. This can only be deliberate, even though the reasons and basis for such selectivity are not yet understood.

The famed Egyptologist, Schwaller de Lubicz, was able, in his research, to show that there was a rational system in the dismantling and rebuilding processes. Certain blocks from an old temple were placed beneath the columns of a new temple, as if it was the seed to nourish a new plant.

In his view, the temple had its natural, organic lifetime, and when the temple had completed its predestined cycle it was torn down, or revised, or added to. Even though he could not show exactly what these cycles were or how they were determined, he found much interesting evidence to support his idea, throughout Egypt.

Many other scholars have accepted that the re-deployment of blocks was deliberate, and that the purpose of this re-deployment was to regenerate the new temple.

The works of the "Great Criminal Akhenaton", so named by the ancient Egyptians, were razed to the ground. His case does not apply to monument appropriation. His story will be told in later chapters.

We have two interesting cases to review:
1) Ramses II (1304-1237 BCE), the greatest builder of all Egypt, was also the greatest "appropriator." The "appropriations" of Rames II pose many questions. Sometimes,

Ramses cut the names of his predecessors out and inserted his own, but in other instances he did not. Sometimes he completed work begun by a previous king, and gave that king appropriate credit. In many instances, when he did "appropriate" a temple, he also left many of the prior cartouches untouched and plainly visible. Yet in other cases, he altered all the cartouches.

2) When Tuthomosis III (1490-1436 BCE) came to power, one of his acts was to erect a high wall around Hatshepsut's obelisk at the Karnak Temple, that hid only its lower two-thirds and left its top third visible for miles.

The common simplistic explanation for such an action is that it was cheaper to hide the bottom two-thirds of its height than removing it. But building a wall around an obelisk leaving the top 4.6m (15ft) visible for 80 km (50 mi) does not make sense. Tuthomosis, the mighty king, could certainly have pulled down an obelisk in the blink of an eye if he wanted to. There has to be a better explanation for this wall.

In certain instances, Hatshepsut's name has been left intact in full view of one and all. In other instances, it has been erased from hidden, dark, inaccessible shrines.

At Hatshepsut's commemorative temple in western Luxor, two images of Hatshepsut are left intact. Also in the **Het-Heru**(*Hathor*) sanctuary, one can see Hatshepsut and Tuthomosis III kneeling; she is holding an offering of milk and he is holding one of wine. There is no defacement there.

It is the selectivity of the damage that has baffled and fascinated the scholars for centuries. There must be a certain rationale to all these apparent appropriations, that we are unaware of.

The Pyramids of Egypt

There are numerous structures which have/had the shape of a pyramid. The genuine pyramids, however, are those which consist of *solid core masonry*. There are only ten such genuine pyramids.

They are located within 80 km (50 mi) of each other. They were all built during the Third and Fourth Dynasties (2630-2472 BCE). In a little more than a century, twenty-five million tons of limestone was used to build these pyramids.

Later, ungenuine pyramids were built during the Fifth and later Dynasties. They were built of loose stone rubble and sand, sandwiched between stone walls. Most are now little more than heaps of rubble, because this type of construction rapidly deteriorates, once the casing is badly damaged or removed.

The Ten Solid Masonry Pyramids Are:
(Location Map on page 105)

1. Zoser's [Step] Pyramid *at Saqqara*.
2. Sekhemket's [Unfinished Step] Pyramid *at Saqqara*.
3. Kha-ba's Layer Pyramid *at Zawyet el Aryan*.
4. Huni and/or Snefru Pyramid *at Meidum*.
5. Snefru's Bent Pyramid *at Dahshur*.
6. Snefru's Red Pyramid *at Dahshur*.
7. Khufu's(*Cheops* in Greek) Great Pyramid *at Giza*.
8. Djedefra's (Unfinished) Pyramid *at Abu-Rawash*.
9. Khafra's(*Chephren* in Greek) Pyramid *at Giza*.
10. Menkaura's(*Mycerinus*) Pyramid *at Giza*.

Why the Stone Pyramids Are Not Tombs

As we will find later in Saqqara, Zoser (2630-2611 BCE) built complete underground burial chambers, for himself and his family. The stepped pyramid was built later. The burial chambers are not an integral part of the pyramid structure, i.e. the first pyramid was an after-thought.

The other nine remaining pyramids, which have been constructed from solid core masonry, are not tombs. These nine solid masonry pyramids, after Zoser's, contain a total of fourteen uninscribed rooms and just three empty, uninscribed stone chests, incorrectly referred to as *sarcophagi*.

The following are the major differences between the pyramids and Egyptian tombs, throughout its long history:

Firstly, these nine pyramids are totally void of ANY official inscriptions, offering rooms, and other funerary features, found in both earlier and later tombs.

Secondly, there are too few empty "stone chests" and too many empty rooms in these nine pyramids, to theorize that they were tombs.

Thirdly, the passageways in the nine pyramids are too narrow to provide for the manipulation of the stone chests. These nine pyramids are distinctively lacking adequate space arrangements.

Fourthly, if we accept, hypothetically, that robbers might have smashed the stone chests and their lids, one can hardly accept the logic that these robbers would have taken the trouble to steal the smashed stone chests.

In spite of careful search, no chips of broken stone chests or their lids were found anywhere in the pyramids' passages and chambers.

Fifthly, one pharaoh, Snefru (2575-2551 BCE) built two and maybe even three pyramids, and nobody expects him to be buried in all three of them.

Lastly, no human remains were ever found inside the nine masonry pyramids. Thieves steal treasures, but they would

Understanding Ancient Egyptians

naturally avoid dead bodies.

As you review the sites and interiors of these pyramids, in later chapters, you will discover the overwhelming evidence that the pyramids were not built to entomb anybody.

The All-Egyptian Story (Isis & Osiris)

It is an incredible fact that there is not a single complete Egyptian record of the *Isis(Auset)* & *Osiris(Ausar)* legend, probably because it was so common to all Egyptians.

Our knowledge of this legend comes from several versions that were written by the Greek and Roman writers of classical antiquity. These writers relied on second or third-hand information, and possibly added their own personal flavours to appeal to their own readers at home. It is therefore impossible to determine which portions of the story are true and which are fabrications.

The common version, was that *Ausar(Osiris)* married *Auset(Isis)*, and *Set(Seth)* married *Nebt-het(Nephthys)*. *Ausar(Osiris)* became King of Egypt, at which time the Egyptians were a totally uncivilized people.

Ausar taught Egyptians the arts of agriculture and irrigation. He showed them how to build houses and gave them laws and education and even the skill of writing, using the hieroglyphic script that was invented by *Tehuti(Thoth)*.

Auset supported her husband in every way. Both *Ausar* and *Auset* were adored by their subjects. But their evil brother *Set* hated *Ausar* and was jealous of his popularity. *Set* managed to pick a fight with *Ausar*, murdered him, and cut his body into fourteen pieces, which he scattered all over Egypt. *Ausar*'s faithful wife, *Auset*, found every part of her husband's body, except the phallus, which had been swallowed by a fish. She assembled his body, making the first Egyptian mummy.

At the time of his death, *Ausar* and *Auset* had no children, but by mystical means, *Ausar* was resurrected for one night and slept with **Auset**. As a result, **Auset** conceived a son. He was called **Heru**(*Horus*) and was raised secretly in the marshes of the Delta to protect him from his evil uncle.

Ausar was resurrected as a soul to rule the Netherworld. **Ausar** became for the Egyptians the spirit of the past, the **neter** of the Dead and a hope for resurrection and after-life.

After **Ausar**'s death, **Set** became the King of Egypt and ruled as a tyrant.

As soon as **Heru** had grown to manhood, he challenged his evil uncle, **Set**, for the right to the throne. After many battles and challenges, **Heru** eventually overcame **Set**, avenged the murder of his father, and regained the throne of Egypt. **Heru** became a role model, the type of perfect Pharaoh. Subsequently, all other rulers used the name **Heru** as one of their official titles, throughout the Egyptian history.

The Pharaohs identified themselves with **Heru** as a living king (conscience, will) and with the soul of **Ausar** as a dead king (sub-conscience).

During the battle, **Set** snatched away the eye of **Heru**, and threw it into the celestial ocean. **Tehuti** recovered the eye which was later called the Utchat-Eye. It was identified with the moon and became a very popular symbol of protection. It was this Eye which **Heru** used to revive his sleeping father.

Another version of the story indicates that as soon as she heard of this tragedy, **Auset** set out to search for the fragments of her husband's body, embalmed them with the help of the **Neter Anpu**(*Anubis*), and buried them wherever they were found. According to this version of the story, the head of **Ausar** was buried at **Abtu**(*Abydos*). The heart was buried on the island of Philae, near Aswan. The phallus was thrown into the Nile and was swallowed by a fish.

Egyptian Art – The Cube

The Egyptian was highly conscious of the box-like structure, which is the model of the earth or the material world. During the Middle Kingdom, the form of statuary, called the *"cube statue"* was initiated. The subject was integrated into the cubic form of the stone. In some of these cube statues, there is a powerful sense of the subject emerging from the prison of the cube. Its symbolic significance could possibly be that the spiritual principle is

emerging from the material world.

Man, in his/her earthly existence, is placed inside the cube. The Divine person is shown sitting squarely on a cube i.e. mind over matter.

Other traditions such as the Platonic and Pythagorean, adopted the same concept of the Egyptian cubic representation of the material world.

The Egyptian temple was designed as a model of the universe at its creation, which is the cube. The contiguous planes of this cubical environment were carefully defined as separate entities, and are to be found in the fully developed Egyptian temple.

The careful definition of the separate planes of this cubic universe is revealed in an art, which is essentially two dimensional. In order to represent three-dimensional objects on a plane surface, the Egyptians avoided the perspectival solution of the problem. That resulted in a two-dimensional profile with the exception of a few parts of the body, like the eyes and sometimes the horns.

The Egyptian Calendars

Egypt worked according to an extremely accurate triple calendar. Each calendar has its own purpose. Egypt planned separate festivals according to all three calendars. They were:

1- A lunar calendar of alternating twenty-nine and thirty-day months.
2- A civil calendar of 360 days plus five additional days (on which the *neteru* were said to be born).
3- A calendar of slightly over 365¼ days based upon the heliacal return of the star Sirius.

During the very remote periods of the ancient Egyptian history, *Auset(Isis)* was associated with the star Sirius (the brightest star in the night sky), who was called, like her, the Great Provider, and whose annual rising ushered in the Nile's annual inundation and the beginning of the Egyptian Year. It occurred when Sirius rose on the horizon together with the sun, and remained visible for a few moments until it faded with the advance of dawn. We refer to this, as the heliacal rising of Sirius (from Greek *helios*, "*the sun*"). This fact is clearly acknowledged in the Webster dictionary, which defines the Sothic (*Sopdit* in Egyptian) year as:

- of having to do with Sirius, the Dog Star.
- Designating or of an ancient Egyptian cycle or period of time based on fixed year of 365¼ days (Sothic Year) and equal to 1,460 such years.

The length of the Sothic year was computed from one rising of the Dog Star (Sirius) to another. But the annual rising of Sirius was not the beginning of the year, because

Understanding Ancient Egyptians

Sirius appears to move in a spiral orbit, from one year to the next.

The Egyptians regarded Sirius as the great central fire, for our sun. Sirius' precise cosmic role, in our *modern* astronomy and physics, is still unfolding. Some modern scholars suspect that Egypt knew that Sirius is the greater sun, about which our sun and solar system orbits.

Egypt's ingenious and very accurate calendar was based on the observation and the study of Sirius' movements in the sky.

The ancient Egyptians knew that the year was slightly over 365¼ days. The earth takes 365.25636 days to complete one revolution around the sun. The ancient Egyptians were completely aware of this fact, as evidenced at the Abu Simbel Temple of Ramses II, as detailed in a later chapter, at the Abu Simbel site. Located at the back of its sanctuary, 55 m (180 ft) away from the only opening to the Abu Simbel Temple, is a statue of Ramses II, among other statues. The rays of the sun have illuminated his statue, next to Amen's statue, on February 22 (Ramses' coronation day) of each year for more than 3,200 years. The difference, between 365.25 days (as per our modern-day calendar) and 365.25636 days, over a span of 3,200 years, is 20 days. If such a minute difference of 0.00636 (365.25636 - 365.25) days per year was not accounted for, the date of illumination of the statue would have changed, from its original date, many years ago. The illumination of the Ramses II statue has been perfect for all these 3,200 years, because they knew the exact length of the year to a level of accuracy as high, if not higher, than we do nowadays. Moreover, they were able to construct a monument with perfect precision, to match their perfect calculations.

For information on research being done by the Tehuti Research Foundation, to further understand the REAL ancient Egyptians, visit the website, http://www.egypt-tehuti.com.

8. Cairo & Vicinities

*This chapter will include the sites that you can visit while staying in a hotel in the Greater Cairo area, which includes Cairo, Giza, **Men-Nefer**(Memphis), Saqqara, Dahshur, Meidum, the Nile Delta, and the Suez Canal.*

Greater Cairo Area

Cairo is at the crossroads of all traffic to and from the three continents of Asia, Africa, and Europe. Therefore, the Egyptian people have always been aware of, and familiar with, foreigners from many different lands, and have always been the most gracious hosts.

The Cairo today still holds many links to the past, which are evident everywhere. In addition to very modern life amenities, you will see mud-brick homes. You may have to be awakened early by the call of the rooster, living on the roof of the apartment building next to yours. Some of these same people may pull a cell phone out of their pocket, or have a personal computer in their living room.

Cairo isn't as difficult to navigate as you might first think. Just remember to always keep an eye out for traffic, bicycles, donkey carts, motorcycles, etc, coming from all sides, and also remember that the people are more kind and polite than most other large cities.

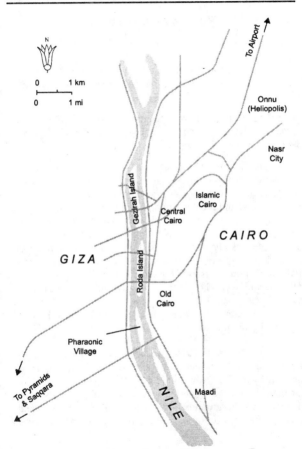

Greater Cairo Area

Points of Interest

Pharaonic Sites

• *The Pyramids and Sphinx* are located 15 km (9 mi) west of Cairo, in Giza. *(see the Giza section, for more details)*

• *The Step Pyramid*, at Saqqara, 32 km (20 mi) south of Giza, is the world's first great stone structure. *(see the Saqqara section for more details)*

• *The Egyptian Museum (page 87)*, near Tahrir Square, downtown, contains more than 100,000 artifacts from over 3,000 years of ancient Egyptian history. You will find the King Tutankhamun exhibit on the second floor, as well as the mummy exhibit (if open). It costs an extra EP10 to use your camera (no flashes) in the museum; otherwise, you can leave your camera safely at the guard station. The museum is poorly lit, so higher speed film is recommended. You will need to pay much more to use your video camera. There are official guides available, who can take you around for a reasonable rate.

The museum is open daily from 9am to 4pm and Fridays, 9am to 11:15am and 1.30pm to 4pm.

• *The Pharaonic Village (page 85)* is a great place for the whole family to view a reanactment of the daily of life of ancient Egyptians. You ride in a boat, and gently float along a canal, to view the scenes, acted out by young students. Also available on the grounds, are a restaurant, papyrus museum, photographs of you in ancient Egyptian attire, and a decent gift shop.

• *Heliopolis(**Onnu**)* (page 85) - This eastern suburb of

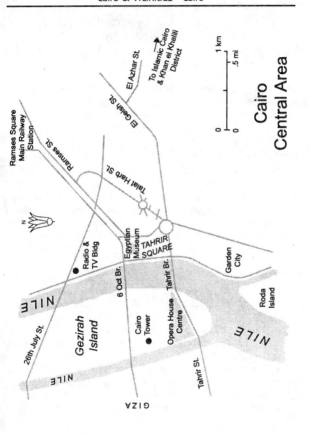

Cairo, was named Heliopolis (City of the Sun) by the Greeks. It was the chief site for the worship/study of **Ra**. The ancient Egyptians called this place **Onnu**. It was an important cultural centre, and was one of ancient Egypt's four cosmological centres. [The other three are **Men-Nefer**(*Memphis*), **Khmunu**(*Hermopolis*), and **Ta-Apet**(*Thebes*)]. **Onnu** was totally destroyed by later generations. A single standing obelisk is the only reminder of **Onnu**'s greatness.

Christian Sites (*page 85*)

- **El Mouallaqa Church**, meaning 'the hanging Church', is next to the Coptic Museum in Old Cairo. It was built by the Romans in the 1st century.
- **The Coptic Museum**, in Old Cairo, contains rare collections dating back to the early Christian era. Open daily from 9am to 4pm. Summer hours 9am to 1pm.

Islamic Sites (*page 85*)

- **The Citadel of Salah El-Din** is located in eastern Cairo, at the foot of the Mukattam Hill. This is a 13th century fortress. One of its buildings is the Mohamed Ali Mosque.
- **Mosque of Ibn Tulon**, is distinguished by the external staircase that winds around the minaret. This mosque dates from 879 CE.
- **The Mosque of Sultan Hassan**, Salah El-Din Square, built in the 14th century, is Cairo's largest mosque with the tallest minaret.
- **Al Azhar Mosque**, El-Hussein Square, founded in the 10th century CE.
- **Islamic Museum**, Ahmed Maher Square, contains an entire range of Islamic art, which has been collected from all parts of the Moslem world. Open daily from 9am to 4pm and Fridays, 9am to 11:15am and 1:30pm to 4pm.

Modern Sites

National Cultural Centre (Opera House)   *(page 87)*

This is a new seven storey opera house, located at the Gezirah Exhibition Grounds. It is equipped with the most sophisticated audio-visual system. It includes three theatres:

1. *The Main Theatre* - a closed hall with 1200 seats, and is used for opera, ballet, and classic music performances.

2. *The Second Theatre* - also a closed hall, containing 500 seats, and is used for various events including film festivals and conferences.

3. *The Third Theatre* - an open one with 1000 seats.

The main music hall and opera house have hosted groups from all over the world. There's always something happening here; check Cairo Today and the Egyptian Gazette for the latest details. Jackets and ties are required for men, and women should dress appropriately.

Cairo Tower (Gezirah)   *(page 87)*

This tower is over 180 m (590 ft) high, and easy to spot, near the Cultural Centre. The observation platform at the top is a good place to view Cairo, from all sides, and the rotating restaurant offers a sumptuous meal.

Cairo International Centre for Conference   *(page 85)*

Located in Nasr City, in northern Cairo. It contains three main conference halls, a fourth for receptions and a fifth for exhibitions. In addition, there are fully-equipped secretarial offices and a press centre.
- Main Hall: 2,500 sq m (27,000 sq ft), 2,500 seats.
- Second Hall: 840 sq m (9,000 sq ft), 800 seats.
- Third Hall: 900 sq m (9,700 sq ft), 600 seats.
- Receptions Hall: 1,600 sq m (17,000 sq ft), 1,250 seats.
- Exhibition Hall: 2,500 sq m (27,000 sq ft).

The Giza Plateau

(Location Map on page 105)

The Giza district begins on the west side of the river Nile, opposite Cairo. You probably won't even notice when you arrive into Giza.

Once you arrive at the Giza Pyramids, you'll pay an admission fee, to permit you to:
• walk around the area
• enter pyramids (excluding the Pyramid of **Khufu**(*Cheops*))
• view the Sphinx and its Temple.

Admission to tour the Solar Boat Museum is extra, and worth the effort, if you have the time.

The pyramid site is open from 8am to 4:30pm daily, but the interior chambers close around 3.30pm.
The best times to visit and photograph the area, are at sunrise and sunset.

Camel and Horse Rides

Some tourists feel almost an obligation to ride a camel or horse at the pyramids - it's one of those touristy things that everybody back home expects you to do.

If you choose to do it, ask a tour guide, or someone else, about the going rates and conditions. Then, approach one of the drivers waiting around. Finalize the price before you come close to the animal, and don't show your excitement. Make sure you know everything the price (in EGYPTIAN pounds - not just *pounds*) includes, so there are no surprises later on.

The behaviour and extortion/over-charging of these camel drivers, is a disgrace to Egyptians.

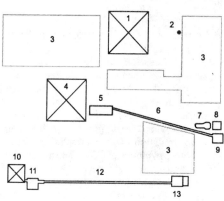

1 - Great Pyramid of Khufu (Cheops)
2 - Tomb of Hetepheres (Khufu's mother)
3 - Mastaba Fields
4 - Pyramid of Khafra (Chephren)
5 - Pyramid Temple of Khafra (Chephren)
6 - Causeway to Valley Temple
7 - Great Sphinx
8 - Temple of the Sphinx
9 - Valley Temple of Khafra (Chephren)
10 - Pyramid of Menkaura (Mycerinus)
11 - Pyramid Temple of Menkaura (Mycerinus)
12 - Menkaura (Mycerinus) Causeway
13 - Valley Temple of Menkaura (Mycerinus)

Giza Plateau

Pyramid of Khufu(Cheops) (2551-2528 BCE)

You have to buy an extra ticket from the kiosk near the **Khufu**(*Cheops*) Pyramid, to enter it.

The Main Components of the Interior Include:

1. Ascending Passage: After passing through the entrance, this passage rises at an angle of 26 degrees for a distance of 39m (129ft). The passage is too low for someone to walk upright - one must go through it hunched over.

The unnecessary smallness of this passage is contrary to all Egyptian tombs, where ample passages or shafts are provided for the manipulation of the sarcophagus. The Great Pyramid and all other pyramids of Giza, Dahshur and Meidum are distinctively lacking in such space arrangements.

At the end of the ascending passage, there are two passages, one continues horizontally and ends at the "Queen's Room", while the other one is the famous Grand Gallery which leads us to the "King's Room".

2. Grand Gallery: Like all internal passages, its angle of ascension is 26 degrees. It is 48m (157ft) long, 8.5m (29ft) high and 1.6m (62in) wide at the bottom and 1m (41in) wide at the top.

Egyptian tombs always contained figures of *neteru*(*gods/goddesses*), offerings or inscriptions, which are all noticeably absent here, as well as the above-mentioned pyramids.

Once inside the gallery, especially at its top, one can envision this gallery open to the sky, acting as an astronomical observatory.

The passage leads to a side room which consists of a short constricted passageway for several feet, and then opens into the "King's Room".

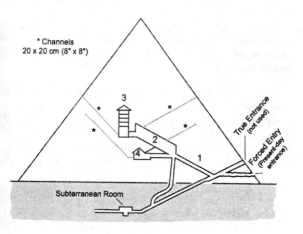

Height (Original):	147m (481ft)
Base:	230m (754ft) square
Mass:	6.5 million tons of solid limestone
Area of Base:	5.3 hectares (13 acres)

Khufu's Pyramid

3. "King's Room": The passageway leading from the top end of the Grand Gallery to the "King's Room", contains distinctive features. The passageway <u>is too narrow for the empty, uninscribed, lidless granite chest, that is now in the "King's Room", to pass through it.</u> This means that the granite chest was placed in the room, as the pyramid was being built.

Even though the top of the granite chest is grooved to accommodate a lid, no lid, or remains of a lid, have been found in any of the pyramid passages or rooms, in spite of careful research.

If this room was used for the dead Pharaoh's, they must have dragged his dead body up these difficult passages so as to squeeze him through the narrow constrictions to his final resting place! Does anybody really believe that could have happened?! If that happened, then later his mummy was somehow stolen (?!), while the pyramid was totally sealed from the outside. (?!)

☞ The "King's Room" got its name from the Arabs, because their men were usually buried in tombs with a flat roof and their women in rooms with a gabled roof. So, in the Great Pyramid, the flat-roofed granite room was called the "King's Room" while the gabled, limestone room was called the "Queen's Room".

4. "Queen's Room": The horizontal passage, from the top of the ascending passage to this room, is 39m (127ft) long. At the end of this passage, the floor suddenly drops 60cm (2ft). No explanation was given by any scholar as to the purpose of such a drop.

☞ There are not, and never were, inscriptions or illustrations anywhere in the passages and rooms of the pyramid.

The Exteriors of the Pyramids

The pyramid's core was built mostly of limestone blocks. The core masonry was originally faced with fine-grained limestone, which was angled to produce the slope of the pyramid.

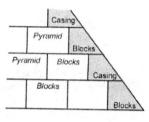

The four sloping faces of the Khufu pyramid were originally dressed with 115,000 casing stones, 5.5 acres of them, on each of its four faces. Each casing stone weighs ten to fifteen tons apiece. The Greek historian, Herodotus, stated that the joints between them were so finely dressed, as to be nearly invisible. A tolerance of 0.25mm (0.01") was the maximum allowed between these stones, so that even a piece of paper cannot fit between them.

The casing blocks, in all pyramids, are made of fine-grained limestone that appears to be polished, and which would have shone brilliantly in the Egyptian sun. The casing blocks of this and most other pyramids, was removed and used to build mosques, after the 640 CE Arab/Moslem invasion of Egypt.

Khufu Boat Museum

This museum is located next to Khufu's Pyramid, and contains one of Khufu's boats, that were placed next to his pyramid. It is made of cedar wood, and is in very good condition. The boat is larger and more seaworthy than Columbus' Mayflower ship. There are water marks on it, indicating that it was used. The museum is open from 9-4 daily, and a special ticket is required to visit it. Slip-on shoe protectors are provided at the entrance, to reduce dust inside.

Pyramid of *Khafra*(*Chephren*) (2520-2494 BCE)

Khafra's pyramid is the most preserved pyramid of the Giza group; it stands close to Khufu's, and in size is almost its twin, for two reasons:

1) It was built on a slightly higher ground than Khufu's.
2) It maintained its summit, while Khufu's pyramid lost its top 10 m (33ft).

The Interior of Khafra's Pyramid

• There are two entrances, one directly above the other, leading into the pyramid. The upper passage, 15m (50ft) above ground, is the one we use to enter the pyramid. This narrow polar passage descends at a 25° 55' angle, down into the bedrock. It levels off, and then continues horizontally to a large limestone room. The walls of the sloping section and part of the horizontal section are lined with red granite, for unknown reasons. The passages are totally void of any inscriptions.

• The only room, in this pyramid, is hewn out of the rock, and roofed with gabled limestone slabs. These slabs are set at the same angle as the pyramid face. It is totally void of any inscriptions. There is an empty uninscribed, beautiful, polished granite box. The box is set into the floor of the room, up to the level of the lid. When the pyramid was first entered, in 1818 CE, the granite box was found, empty and clean, with the lid broken into two pieces, next to the box.

Khafra Pyramid Complex

The *Khafra* Pyramid is connected to the following:

• Remains of *Khafra*'s(*Chephren*'s) Pyramid (wrongly known as *mortuary*) Temple.

• The causeway between the Temple of Khafra and the Valley Temple, which is 500 m (1650 ft) long.

• The Valley Temple of Khafra is a simple but massive structure with no inscriptions whatsoever. Later excavations found statues of Khafra in a pit in this temple.

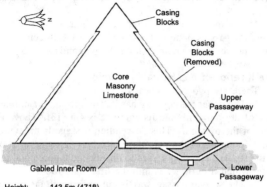

Height: 143.5m (471ft)
Base: 214.5m (708ft) square
Mass: 5.3 million tons of solid limestone
Angle: 53° 7' 48"

Interior of Khafra's Pyramid

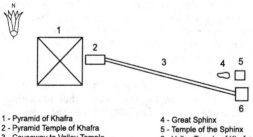

1 - Pyramid of Khafra
2 - Pyramid Temple of Khafra
3 - Causeway to Valley Temple
4 - Great Sphinx
5 - Temple of the Sphinx
6 - Valley Temple of Khafra

Profile of Causeway

Pyramid of Menkaura (Mycerinus) (2494-2472 BCE)

This is the smallest pyramid of the three at Giza. Extensive damage was done to the exterior, by a 16th century caliph who decided to demolish all the pyramids.

The Interior of Menkaura's Pyramid

There are two passageways:

1) The upper passageway has its entrance on the northern face of the pyramid, and its entrance is 4m (13ft) above the base of the pyramid. This descending passage is the typical polar (pointing to the celestial pole) type, measuring about 31m (102ft). The sloping section leads into a horizontal passage, which in turn, leads into the first inner room.

2) The second passageway is cut underneath the original upper passageway. The lower passageway is the one we use to enter the pyramid and it is lined with granite. It is also pointing to the celestial pole. The lower passage leads westward to a staircase, then down to a room containing six niches (called the *Celled Room*.) Still further west, lies the main underground room.

This room is cut out of the bedrock, and is entirely lined with red granite and totally void of any inscriptions.

Its ceiling appears to be vaulted, a perfect barrel vault, but on closer examination, you will find that the ceiling is actually formed of large, tightly fitted granite slabs, laid in facing gables.

This room contained a single basalt chest, with no inscriptions whatsoever. The chest was carried out earlier this century, to be shipped to England, but was lost at sea, off the Spanish coast.

Outside, are the excavated remains of Menkaura's Pyramid (wrongly known as mortuary) Temple and, further east, the ruins of his valley temple, still lying beneath the sand.

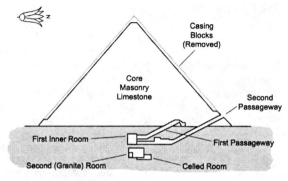

Base: 108m (356ft) square
Height: 67m (218ft)
Mass: 0.6 million tons of solid limestone

Cross Section of Menkaura's Pyramid

The End of the Pyramid Age

Menkaura Pyramid was the last genuine stone pyramid. Shepseskaf (2472-2467 BCE) followed Menkaura, and built what is commonly known as Mastabat Fara'un, located in Southern Saqqara. After Shepseskaf died, the Fourth Dynasty ended. The kings of the Fifth Dynasty paid attention to their funeral complexes, but the pyramids that they built were just heaps of rubble.

The inner structures of these later ungenuine pyramids have the normal spacious passages, offering rooms and other funerary features found in both earlier and later tombs. There is not the slightest doubt that these later structures were built to serve as tombs, and nothing but tombs.

The Sphinx

The Sphinx is about 70m (230ft) long, and 20m (65ft) high. Many say that Khafra carved the Sphinx somewhere between 2520-2494 BCE. But these commonly held beliefs are questionable. Let us study the evidence...

The original site, where the Sphinx is located, was a gently sloping plane with an outcrop of harder rock. The head of the Sphinx was carved out of this outcrop.

To form the body of the Sphinx, the stone had been quarried away, from all around the soon-to-be body. So, we have:

A- *The head of the Sphinx* was made of a hard strata which is resistant to the effects of the natural elements. The present damage to the face was caused by soldiers who used the Sphinx as an artillery target in the eighteenth century.

B- *The body of the Sphinx* was made of a softer limestone strata which in turn consists of alternate harder and softer layers. These alternate layers are visible on site as weathered corrugation, which is about two feet deep into the bedrock. Most scholars agree that this erosion pattern is a result of a single event.

C- *The base of the Sphinx*, which is also the bottom of the original quarry site, is made of a harder limestone that is resistant to the effects of the natural elements.

Since the Sphinx has been covered by sand, from the time it was created thousands of years ago, it was actually protected from natural elements. The concave shape of the erosion is not the result of wind action. It was therefore concluded that the erosion to the body of the Sphinx was caused by water, in a single event. But what was that single event that caused the erosion? It was suggested by some, that ground water may have risen, through capillary action, to react with the limestone of the Sphinx body causing this one-time erosion event. After 500 years the ground water dropped back down, and this phenomenon was never to occur again!

The evidence is overwhelming against the ground water theory. Here is why:

A - It is estimated that the ground water table was 9m (30ft) lower in *Khafra*'s time than its present level. It is impossible for the ground water:

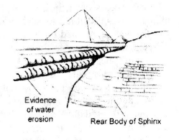

(i) to rise from a much deeper level than its present level.
(ii) to erode 60cm (2ft) deep channels into the body of the Sphinx, and the walls of the quarry pit, in the span of five hundred years.
(iii) to drop, after this 500 years, and not to occur again.

B- Additionally, why didn't this ground water theory have any effect at the following places:

(i) The bedrock of the quarry pit where the Sphinx rests? This area was never eroded and therefore was naturally never repaired.
(ii) All the structures built during the Old Kingdom, and there are scores of them throughout the country?

C- The Pyramid (wrongly known as *"Mortuary"*) Temple of *Khafra* stands 46m (150ft) above the plateau and had a similar erosion pattern to the body of the Sphinx. There was definitely no ground water in the case of this temple.

The only logical answer is that the water erosion occurred at the end of the last Ice Age, c. 15,000-10,000 BCE.

Khafra, Builder or Restorer of the Sphinx

The writers of antiquity mentioned the Sphinx without attributing it to any particular Pharaoh. King Tuthomosis IV (1413-1405 BCE) established a stele and placed it between the paws of the Sphinx. It is a long text, but the name of *Khafra* appears on it, in hieroglyphs. The text surrounding the name was illegible. As such, no one knows why the name *Khafra* was mentioned on this stele.

A graphic outline to the same scale of both *Khafra* and the Sphinx' head was made and both were superimposed on each other, on a U.S. Television network and there was no resemblance between the two whatsoever.

Academic Egyptologists also chose to dismiss an important piece of evidence, namely the "Inventory Stele" which was found in Giza, in the nineteenth century.

This stele describes events during the reign of *Khufu*, *Khafra*'s predecessor, and indicates that *Khufu* ordered the building of a "monument" alongside the Sphinx. This means that the Sphinx was already there before *Khufu*, and therefore could not have been built by his son, *Khafra*. The stelae was dismissed by some, because its stylistic features appeared to be from the New Kingdom. Even though there are many steles and texts from the Old Kingdom that were, like this stele, copied (similar to reprinting a book) in the New Kingdom and no one dismissed them on such a basis.

The overwhelming physical evidence, as detailed above, leads us to the rational conclusion that *Khafra* did not and could not have built the Sphinx.

The found statues of *Khafra* at the Valley Temple, the mention of *Khafra*'s name on Tuthomosis IV's stele, and *Khafra*'s causeway may lead us to the conclusion that *Khafra* was probably one of the restorers of the Sphinx, which was damaged at the end of the last Ice Age.

Sound & Light Show

There is open-air seating on the terrace at the *Khufu(Cheops)* Pavilion, near the Sphinx and facing *Khafra(Chephren)*'s valley temple. The Sphinx takes the role of the narrator, in this Sound & Light Show.

There are three shows every evening with various languages scheduled for different nights of the week, as follows:

Winter	6:30pm	7:30pm	8:30pm
Summer	8:30pm	9:30pm	10:30pm
Monday	English	French	Spanish
Tuesday	English	Italian	French
Wednesday	English	French	German
Thursday	Japanese	English	Arabic
Friday	English	French	
Saturday	English	Spanish	Italian
Sunday	Japanese	French	German

Entrance fee is EP 30 plus EP 3 sales tax. Private shows for 50 or more people, are available with prior arrangement. For further information, contact Misr Co. for Sound & Light, Cairo (Tel: 385 2880, 386 5469, Fax: 384 4259).

Memphis (Men-Nefer)

Memphis is located 24 km (15 mi) southwest of Cairo, in Al-Badrasheen. Memphis is a Greek corruption of the ancient Egyptian *Men-Nefer*, meaning "Established-in-Beauty/Harmony".

During the Old Kingdom, **Men-Nefer** was the capital of Egypt, and was quite reknowned at that time. Herodotus described it as a 'prosperous city and cosmopolitan centre'. **Men-Nefer** never lost its grandeur after the pharaohs of the Middle and New Kingdoms chose **Ta-Apet**(*Thebes*) as their main residence. All these pharaohs continued to receive their education and training in this one of the four cosmological centres in Egypt. The other three are **Onnu**(*Heliopolis*), **Khmunu**(*Hermopolis*), and **Ta-Apet**(*Thebes*).

There isn't much left to remind us of the glory of **Men-Nefer** - only a small museum and some statues. There is a large, but damaged, fine-grained limestone statue of Ramses II in the museum. It is 13m (42ft) high, and weighs 120 tons. There are also an eight ton Alabaster Sphinx of King Tuthomosis III, some alabaster beds for mummifying the Sacred Apis Bulls, and some more statues of Ramses II.

Men-Nefer was the centre for the worship of **Ptah**, the divine architect, and the creative fire. **Ptah** is equivalent to the Greek *Hephaistos*, and the Romans' *Vulcan*.

The Egyptian Coffin Texts, Spell 1130, reads: *"I am the Lord of fire who lives on Truth."* **Ptah** represented the coagulating fire that caused the creation of the world.

Ptah

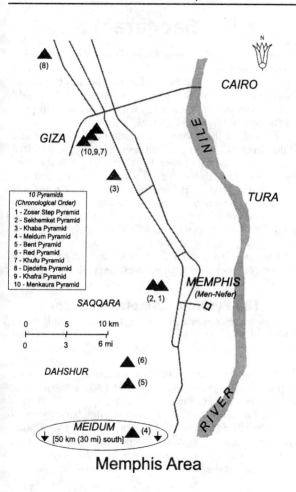

Saqqara

Saqqara is about an hour's drive from Cairo. The origin of the Arabic name, *"Saqqara"*, is derived from the name of the Egyptian **neter**(*god*) **Sekar**(*Sokar*), who was one of the **Men-Nefer** triad: Ptah-Sokar-Nefertum. Saqqara was the main northern necropolis of ancient Egypt, since (and probably prior to) the time of Dynastic Egypt.

Throughout the history of dynastic Egypt, until the end of the Greek rule under the Ptolemies, Saqqara was the place where every important person left their mark. It is therefore a very important archaeological site. Uncovering and discovering important archaeological artifacts goes on, and will continue to go on here, for decades to come.

A worthwhile visit to Saqqara will take more than one day. The sites are open between 7:30am and 4pm.

Here are some quick glances at the major sites, that one can complete in one day, which most tours allow for:

The Pyramid Complex of Zoser

This complex was built during the reign of King Zoser (2630-2611 BCE), by Imhotep, reknowned "Father of Masons", and consists of the following main features:

1 - The Enclosure Wall - When complete, the enclosure wall was nearly 550m (1800ft) long and 300m (985ft) wide, and rose to a height of over 9.1m (30ft).

The Enclosure Wall has 14 bastion gates, but only one is real. The other 13 are simulated. The reason for such simulated gates remains a total mystery. The false doors look quite real, with minute details of hinges and sockets.

The only real entrance leads to the colonnade.

Cairo & Vicinities - Saqqara

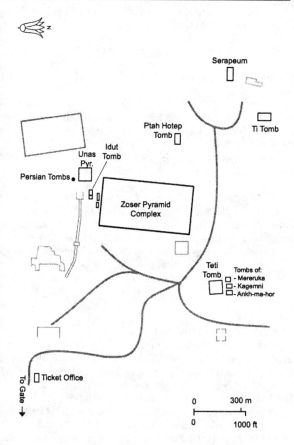

Saqqara (Northern) Site Plan

2 - The Colonnade - There are 40 reeded (like bunches of reeds bound together) columns.

3 - The Southern Tomb - This tomb is 28m (92ft) deep. It has a few chambers which are lined with blue faience tiles. These chambers are too small to hold a mummy.

4 - Heb-Sed Court - During the 30th year of a Pharaoh's reign, it was traditional for him to rejuvenate his rule by re-enacting his coronation rituals, in this court, in what was called the Heb-Sed Festival.

The two stone altars, in the middle of the Great Court, probably had some role in the Heb-Sed festivities.

5 - Northern & Southern Buildings - These buildings represent the shrines of Upper and Lower Egypt. The southern buildings are faced with Doric-type columns. Here, as well as many other places throughout Egypt, the evidence is clear that ancient Egypt fashioned the Doric columns, at least 2,000 years before the Greeks. The Northern Building is similar to its southern counterpart, except that the columns are shaped like stalks of open papyri.

The Zoser Step Pyramid

The original objective of this structure was to build a mastaba-type tomb, to bury the king when he died. Building a step pyramid was an afterthought, that occurred some years later. The mastaba-type tomb is functionally and structurally independent of the later addition of the stepped pyramid.

The *first stage* of construction, was the building of a square stone mastaba 63m x 63m x 8m (206ft x 206ft x 26ft), with an underground burial chamber. The core masonry was made of small stone blocks, laid like bricks. The stone mastaba was faced with fine limestone, which proves that the mastaba

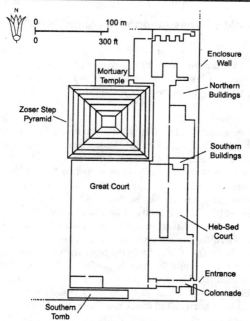

Zoser Pyramid Complex

was intended to be their ultimate goal.

Later, an additional central shaft, a series of corridors and another tomb chamber were also dug, plus about 10m (33ft) widening around the perimeter of the mastaba.

However, a few years later, a six-tiered structure of stone was placed on top of the existing tomb structure, which was, in turn, faced with fine limestone, to give it a smooth finish. The pyramid is now 60m (197ft) high and the bottom rectangular dimensions are 140m x 118m (460ft x 390ft).

Pyramid of Unas (and the "Pyramid Texts")

All the great pyramids of Giza, Dahshur, and Meidum were built during the Fourth Dynasty (2575-2465 BCE), and they have no inscriptions whatsoever, and in every other aspect, differ from other earlier and later tombs, simply because they are not tombs.

One hundred years later, at the end of the Fifth Dynasty, King Unas (2356-2323 BCE), built a small and ungenuine pyramid at Saqqara. The superstructure was nothing more than a heap of rubble, built up to support the outer layers of the core, which in turn, supported the casing stones.

The entry passage to the underground rooms is located on the north side. It leads to an antechamber, then 3 huge granite slabs, and then to the burial chambers, where every centimeter of walls are covered with beautifully executed hieroglyphic texts. Carved into the huge slabs of white alabaster, the texts record the rituals, prayers and hymns that accompanied the Pharaoh's burial. It is these funerary texts, carved on the walls, that are called the '**Pyramid Texts**'. They should have been called the '**Unas Funerary Texts**', because these texts don't exist in any of the true great pyramids.

Nobody is sure about the use of these texts. No one knows when these texts were composed, but everyone who has studied them agrees that for the most part, they date from much earlier times. The **Unas Funerary Texts** form the basis for all subsequent funerary literature in Egypt, such as, The Book of the Coming Forth by Day (known, mistakenly, as The Book of the Dead), The Book of What Is In the Duat (or Underworld), The Book of the Gates, The Book of Caverns, The Litany of Re, The Book of Aker, The Book of Day, and The Book of Night.

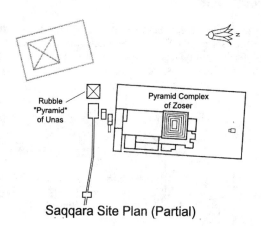

Saqqara Site Plan (Partial)

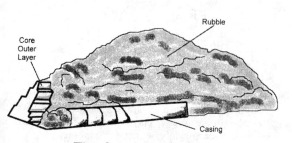

The Superstructure
(Rubble "Pyramid") of Unas

Nobles' Tombs

Saqqara has several beautiful tombs of the nobles and high officials, from the Fifth and Sixth Dynasties (2465-2150 BCE). Each tomb typically consists of an entrance, court(s), corridors, offering rooms, chapel, sacrificial room, and serdab.

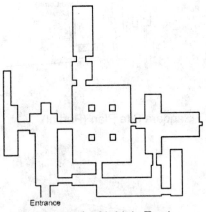

Example of a Noble's Tomb

The main theme in all the Nobles' tombs is similar, yet no two tombs are identical. The walls are covered with various daily life scenes, such as farming, fishing, hunting, sailing, metal-working, music, playing ...etc. These scenes of daily life have deep symbolic metaphysical meanings.

Portraying these daily life activities in the presence of the *neteru*(*gods/goddesses*) or with their assistance signifies their spiritual intent. The agricultural scenes are similar to the symbolism of Christ, referring to the sower of the seed.

It was spiritual and never meant to be agricultural advice.

If you are short of time, visit Idut Tomb, which gives you a brief and complete idea. If you have more time, visit some of the tombs mentioned below. *(Location map on page 107)*

- Tomb of Princess Idut (King Zoser's daughter)
- Tomb of Ti
- Tomb of Ptah-Hotep
- Tomb of Kagemni
- Tomb of Teti
- Tomb of Mereruka
- Tomb of Ankh-ma-hor

Persian Tombs

(Location map on page 107)

These three tombs belonged to high officials, during the Persian rule (525 - 404 BCE). They are the deepest subterranean burial chambers in Egypt, and are beautifully decorated with hieroglyphs.

Serapeum

(Location map on page 107)

The Serapeum is a subterranean complex system of galleries, leading to enormous granite sarcophagi of Apis, 25 of which were embalmed and placed here in huge granite coffins weighing up to 70 tons each.

This Apis catacomb dates from the 13th century BCE, when Ramses II began the first gallery, which reached a length of 67m (220ft). In the 7th century BCE, Psammetichus I cut a new gallery, which was extended by the Ptolemies to a length of 198m (650ft), and used until around 30 BCE.

Because of the dust here, you may need a dust mask. Don't worry if you don't have time to visit the Serapeum.

Mastabat Fara'un (Page 115)

The oldest structure in the south Saqqara area is the unusual structure of Shepseskaf. Pharaoh Shepseskaf (2472-2467 BCE) followed **Menkaura**(*Mycerinus*) to the throne. He did not build a pyramid or a mastaba. Instead, he built a different type of a monument. It was in the shape of a rectangular sarcophagus, 100m x 72m and 20m (328ft x 236ft x 66ft). Arabs called it *Mastabat Fara-un*.

Other points about this monument are:
1.) It did not include any inscriptions whatsoever, and no direct reference to Shepseskaf. References to him are made in nearby tombs.
2.) The underground room is reached via the typical polar passage, pointing to the polar star.
3.) It was never used for Shepsekaf's burial.

Pyramid of Pepi II (Page 115)

A little north of the Mastabat Fara'un is the pyramid of Pepi II (2246-2152 BCE). Yes, he reigned for 94 years. It has been checked so many times, and there is no disagreement among Egyptologists about the length of his reign.

Pepi II's tomb contains some fine hieroglyphs, but the superstructure is and was nothing more than a pile of rubble, like King Unas' structure.

Pepi II was the fourth Pharaoh of the Sixth Dynasty. He was very powerful and very rich and lasted long enough. His memorials are found throughout Egypt as well as various mines and quarries. He had the time and resources to build a pyramid, like those in Giza, Dahshur, and Meidum. Despite all that, he had but this one small ungenuine pyramid.

Trip to Saqqara

The scenery along the road to Saqqara is worth the trip itself.

Cairo & Vicinities - Saqqara

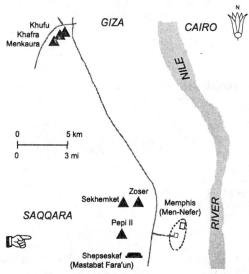

Southern Saqqara & Vicinity

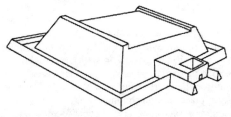

A Reconstruction of Mastabat Fara'un

Dahshur

Snefru's Bent and Red Pyramids are the main attractions in Dahshur.

Snefru's Bent Pyramid (Page 105)

This is the second of three pyramids, built by Snefru (the first is located in Meidum). This pyramid has a unique shape. Its lower half is built at a considerably steeper angle than the top. This stone pyramid is, again, totally void of any markings. This pyramid was attributed to King Snefru (2575-2551 BCE), based on a reference to his name in the nearby temple.

Without any supporting evidence, some think that the two angles of the pyramid were caused by a change in plan. The evidence inside the Bent Pyramid leads us to conclude that its unique double angle was a deliberately planned design. The Bent Pyramid alone has a double-angled profile, and two totally separate sets of rooms, one entrance on the customary north side, pointing to the polar star, and a second entrance on the west side. The early stages of construction reflected that these separate entrances, corridors, and underground rooms were part of the original plan.

The masonry blocks are dressed up with an outer casing, which is still intact.

The Interior of the Bent Pyramid

- The descending passage from the northern entrance is 1.1m (3ft-7in) high, i.e. too low to walk up straight.
- The polar passageway leads to two internal rooms, which have corbel roofs. There is no trace of a stone chest or of a burial taking place in either room.
- A second passage connects the upper room with an opening high up in the western face of the pyramid. This passageway is also 1.1m (3ft-7in) high, i.e. too low.

Cairo & Vicinities - Dahshur   117

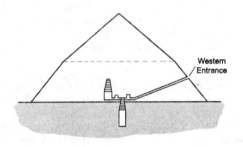

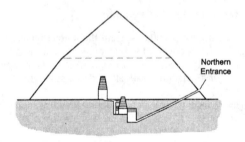

Base: 184m (602ft) square
Height: 105m (344ft)
Mass: 3.6 million tons of solid limestone
Inclination: 53° 27' base
             43° 22' 44" top

Snefru's Bent Pyramid

Snefru's Red Pyramid

(Location map on page 105)

The Red Pyramid is less than 1.5 km (1 mi) north of Snefru's Bent Pyramid. It is the earliest monument which is in complete pyramidical form.

This pyramid looks good because it still retains large areas of its original casing stones.

It is popularly known as the *Red Pyramid* because of the reddish or pinkish tint of its core stones.

This is the third of three pyramids built by Snefru (2575-2551 BCE). Again, there are no inscriptions whatsoever inside or outside of this pyramid.

The Interior of the Red Pyramid

• The entrance passage is again the unique typical polar passage. It leads down a long, sloping corridor, to the bedrock, and is only 1.2m (3ft-11in) high. Again, the passage is too small for a person to walk standing up straight.

• The passage leads to two adjoining identical rooms with corbelled roofs.

• A short passage leads upward to a third large room. The corbelled roof of this third room rises to a height of 15.2m (50ft).

• Here, for the first time, the rooms were incorporated into the pyramid itself (traditionally they were underground).

• No trace of a stone chest or burial was found anywhere in the three rooms.

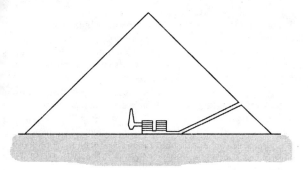

Base: 220m (722ft) square
Height: 104m (34ft)
Mass: 4.0 million tons of solid limestone
Inclination: 43º 22'

Snefru's Red Pyramid

Meidum

(Location map on page 105)

The Pyramid of Meidum is located about 65 km (40 mi) south of Giza. The structure now looks more like kind of a high, stepped tower, rising out of a tremendous heap of rubble. These are the remains of a pyramid. There are no inscriptions indicating who built it. Several graffiti, on and around the ruins, indicate that the Egyptians themselves ascribed it to King Snefru (2575 - 2551 BCE). This is the first of three pyramids built by Snefru.

The original plan of this structure was to build a step pyramid, and was later converted into a true pyramid with smooth sides. It was built in three phases. Each phase was intended to be final, because the exterior walls of each phase, consisted of the typical fine limestone layer.

After the pyramid was completed, a few of the casing blocks were squeezed out of place, a chain reaction followed, and the entire outer casing gave way. Much of the core masonry was pulled with the loose casing stones. As a result of this avalanche, a huge rubble heap was formed around the pyramid, which left portions of the earlier step pyramid intact. This explains its towerlike appearance.

The Interior of the Pyramid of Meidum

• There is only one small room, with no inscriptions, which has a fine corbelled roof (fashioned like steps in reverse).

• Access to the room can only be achieved from the corridor via a narrow vertical shaft. The interior room is set at the top of the shaft. This vertical shaft enters the floor of the room, and is only 117cm x 85cm (3.8ft x 2.8ft) wide.

• When the pyramid was first entered, the room was totally empty. There was never a stone chest there. No granite fragments of a stone chest were found, either in the room itself or anywhere in the corridor.

Cairo & Vicinities - Meidum

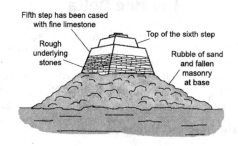

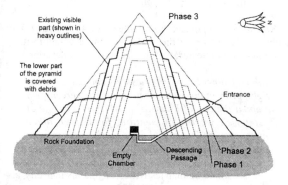

Base (original): 147m (482ft) square
Height (original): 93m (306ft)
Mass (original?): 1.5 million tons of solid limestone
Inclination: 52° 50' 35"

Snefru's Pyramid of Meidum

The Nile Delta

The delta region had an important role in ancient Egypt, as did Upper Egypt. However, most of its archaeological sites were destroyed after 640 CE.

Some archaeological excavations are underway in the Nile Delta, and hopefully more of the ancient Egyptian monuments will be restored.

Zagazig (Ancient Bubastis)

Zagazig is about 80 km (50 mi) northeast of Cairo. The ancient ruins of Bubastis, right outside Zagazig, show one of the most ancient cities in Egypt.

Khufu(Cheops) began this temple in the 4th Dynasty, and numerous pharaohs over the next 17 centuries added to it. It was an architectural gem, that Herodotus described:

"Although other Egyptian cities were carried to a great height, in my opinion the greatest mounds were thrown up about the city of Bubastis, in which is a temple of Bastet well worthy of mention; for though other temples may be larger and more costly, none is more pleasing to look at than this."

The annual festivities of this ancient city attracted more than 700,000 people, singing, dancing, and having a great time. Herodotus described the joy of the people, celebrating Bastet, the symbol of Joy. The cruelty of later generations reduced this marvelous place into a pile of rubble. The cat cemetery - a series of underground galleries - is among the little that survived.

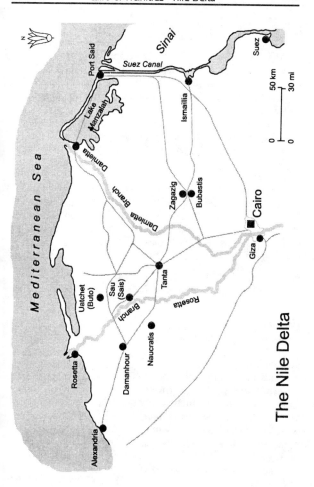

Tanta and Vicinity

(Location map on page 123)

Tanta is located 90 km (56 mi) from Cairo. Tanta is the largest city in the delta. It is an important centre for Sufism. The people's annual celebration of the Sufi saint, Sa-yed El Badawi, resembles in many ways, the ancient Egyptian festivities.

Ther are two ancient sites close by:

Sau(*Sais*)

Sau(*Sais*) was the 26th Dynasty (664 - 525 BCE) capital city of Egypt. *Sau*(*Sais*), however, is as old as the Egyptian civilization. It was the centre of the worship and study of *Net* (*Neith*), who was associated with the Greek *Athena*. It was the place where the Greeks were first allowed to come into Egypt, during the 26th Dynasty. Pythagoras and other Greek notables, came to study in Egypt at this time.

(Buto)*Uatchet*

Uatchet was the focal point, representing Lower Egypt. It was symbolized by the cobra.

The cobra (or uraeus) is the omnipresent protector of all Egypt. Its figure is found everywhere, either alone or together, with *Nekhbet*, the vulture symbol of the South. More about *Nekhbet* on Page 188.

The cobra that can swallow a

huge animal and digest it, was for Egyptians the earthly manifestation of the divine intellect. The faculty of intellect allows a person to break down a whole (complex issue/body) into its constituent parts, in order to digest it.

One of the Egyptian King's titles was, Lord of the diadem of the vulture and of the serpent. The diadem, combining the serpent and vulture, was the earthly symbol of the divine man, the king. The diadem consisted of the *serpent* (symbol of the divisive intellectual function), and the *vulture* (symbol of the reconciliation function). The divine man must be able, both to distinguish and to reconcile. Since these dual powers reside in man's brain, the form of the serpent's body follows the actual physiological sutures of the brain, in which these particularly human faculties are seated.

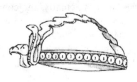

Located in the middle of the forehead, the diadem represents the third eye, with all its intellectual faculties.

The Suez Canal

The Suez Canal connects the Mediterranean Sea with the Gulf of Suez. The Suez Canal is about 163 km (101 mi) long. The canal can accomodate ships as large as 150,000 dead weight tons, fully loaded. The canal has no locks, because the Mediterranean Sea and the Gulf of Suez have roughly the same water level. The canal utilizes three natural bodies of water - Lake Manzalah, Lake Timsah, and the Bitter Lakes (the latter is actually one continuous body of water).

Excavation of the canal was begun on April 25, 1859, and the canal was opened to navigation on November 17, 1869.

About 50 ships a day pass through the canal, at the present time.

The major cities of the Suez Canal are:

Suez

The city of Suez is located on the Red Sea, 132 km (82 mi) east of Cairo, at the southern entrance of the Suez Canal. A favourite fishing and camping spot, Suez is known for the Ataka Mountains along its southern coastline which change colours from pink to purple at different hours of the day.

Ismaillia

Ismaillia is an attractive town, situated on the western shore of Lake Timsah. It was founded by Ferdinand de Lesseps in 1863, and used as his base of operations during the digging of the Suez Canal.

Port Said

Port Said is 217 km (135 mi) northeast of Cairo, at the Mediterranean entrance to the Suez Canal. Port Said has a scenic promenade, running along an attractive beach.

Cairo & Vicinities - Suez Canal 127

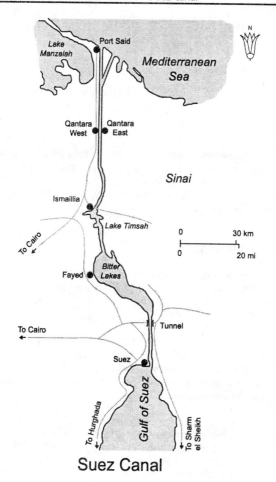

Suez Canal

9. Middle Egypt

El Minya has several hotels, which make this a convenient place, to base yourself for day trips to the tombs and temples of Beni Hasan, Tuna el Gebel, and **Khmunu**(*Hermopolis*). Check with a reliable travel agency, for places to stay, eat, and transportation to the sites.

Beni Hasan

Beni Hasan is located about 25 km (15 mi) south of El Minya. There are 39 Middle Kingdom (2040 - 1783 BCE) tombs, which are carved into the living limestone of the bedrock.

These tombs are very impressive artistically. They also provide clear and explicit scenes of everyday occupations and diversions. There is more emphasis, in these Middle Kingdom tombs, on gymnastics, acrobatics, dance, and wrestling for unknown reasons.

Four of the tombs can be visited:
- Tomb of Amenemhet (No 2)
- Tomb of Khnumhotep (No 3)
- Tomb of Baqet (No 15)
- Tomb of Kheti (No 17)

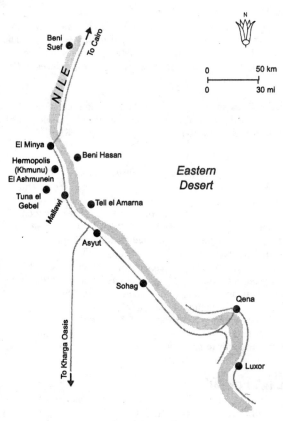

Middle Upper Egypt

Mallawi

Mallawi is 48 km (30 mi) south of El Minya. The name, *Mal-Lawi(Mal-Levi)* means literally, *The City of Levites*. The city still has a small Jewish population. *Mallawi* is a convenient point to reach the ancient sites of *Khmunu(Hermopolis)*, Tuna el Gebel and Tell el Amarna.

Mallawi has an Archaeological Museum that contains a collection of artifacts from Tuna el Gebel and *Khmunu(Hermopolis)*.

Hermopolis(Khmunu) (El Ashumnein)

Khmunu (called *Hermopolis* by the Greeks and *El Ashmunein* by the Arabs) was one of the four cosmological centres in ancient Egypt. [The other three are *Onnu(Heliopolis)*, *Men-Nefer(Memphis)*, and *Ta-Apet(Thebes)*]. *Khmunu* was dedicated to *Tehuti(Thoth)*, The Divine Intellect, wisdom, and writing.

Little remains of this ancient city, which is located 8 km (5 mi) north of Mallawi. The Greeks associated *Tehuti(Thoth)* with their own Hermes, and accordingly the city was called *Hermopolis*. The present-day Arabic name of this ruined city is El Ashmunein - a derivation of *Khmunu*.

All that is left of this great centre, are a few Middle and New Kingdom remains, and a ruined Roman agora.

Tuna el Gebel

Tuna el Gebel was the necropolis of *Khmunu(Hermopolis)*. It is located 10 km (6 mi) from Khmunu. It contains some very interesting tombs, from the Late Kingdom period.

There are also the catacomb galleries filled with mummified baboons, ibises and ibis eggs. Baboons and ibises were sacred to *Tehuti*(*Thoth*).

There are only a very few mummified animals left, due to the pillaging of the tombs.

Tehuti, Master of Khmunu

Tehuti (*Hermes* to the Greeks, *Mercury* to the Romans), was called the Master of the City of Eight (the Ogdoad). This is in reference to the four pairs of primordial deities, that were translated as Night, Obscurity, Secret, and Eternity.

The *neter*(*god*), *Tehuti*(*Thoth*), personifies the divine intellect. He was the messenger of the *neteru*(*gods*), of writing, of language, of knowledge. Tehuti gives man access to the mysteries of the manifested world.

It was *Tehuti*, who uttered the words, commanded by Ra, that created the world. In the Egyptian Book of the Coming Forth by Day (wrongly translated as the Book of the Dead), we read:

Tehuti
(*Thoth*)

> I am the Eternal...I am that which created the Word...I am the Word...

Tehuti is portrayed as an ibis-headed male figure, or sometimes as all ibis. He is also associated with the baboon.

Tell el Amarna

Tell el Amarna is located 12 km (7.5 mi) south of Mallawi, and 40 km (25 mi) south of Beni Hassan. There is nothing left from this site, which was destroyed by Horemheb (1348 - 1335 BCE), who restored the ancient traditions, at the end of the four Amarna Kings (Akhenaton, Semenkhkare, Tutankhamen, and Aye). There is nothing left from Akhenaton's city, except the outline of foundations, and some tombs.

In the 14th century BCE, Akhenaton abandoned *Ta-Apet(Thebes)*, to establish a new capital city. Akhetaton served as the capital of Egypt for about 14 years. It was abandoned for all time shortly after Akhenaton's rule ended.

Contrary to the general view, the name Amarna was not derived from a small Bedouin tribe that settled in the area, in the 19th century. No evidence exists to substantiate that. The name is, however, derived from the name in the second cartouche of Akhenaton's god, namely *Im-r-n*.

The city of Akhetaton was well planned, with temples to Aton, residences for all classes, and tombs for the royal family and their high officials.
The colossal statues of the king and queen surrounded the open courts of the temples.

Viewing the Tombs at Tell el Amarna

The Tell el Amarna tombs are located in the northern and southern areas.

Middle Egypt 133

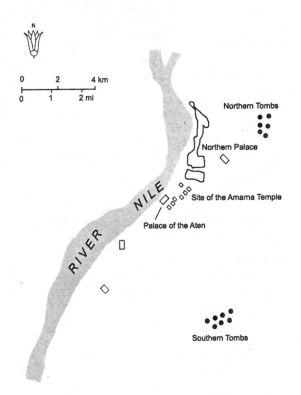

Tell el Amarna Site Plan

Due to the city's sudden demise, many of the tombs were never finished and there is no evidence of burial, or even of sarcophagi, have been found in any of the nobles' tombs.

The main themes in all the tombs repeat themselves. The principal theme in the tombs is not the typical Egyptian daily activity, as in other noble tombs, but the relationship between the deceased and Akhenaton, and other members of the royal family. Sometimes the king is shown as being accessible to his subjects. Other times, the figure of Akhenaton is in place of ***neteru(gods)***.

In Egypt, the king always represented the divine in man. Akhenaton thought that it was he, Akhenaton the man, who was divine.

Akhenaton was never buried in his tomb.

There are five decorated chapels in the northern tombs, that are worth seeing. They are:

Tomb of Huya
Huya was the Steward of Queen Tiye (Akhenaton's mother).

Tomb of Ahmose
Ahmose was an official in the court of Akhenaton's.

Tomb of Meri-re I
Meri-re I was the high priest of Aton.

Tomb of Panhesy
Panhesy was the Chief Servitor.

Tomb of Mari-re II
Meri-re II was the Superintendent of the household of Nefertiti.

The Akhenaton Story

The drama of Akhenaton is the second most controversial subject in Egyptian history, next to the Great Pyramid.

Akhenaton has been called by many 'the first monotheist'. He glorified one of the *neteru*, namely 'Aton', over and above all the other *neteru*(*gods*), but mostly he wanted to challenge Amen and his establishment at *Ta-Apet*(*Thebes*). His vendetta with Amen was motivated as much by politics as by religion.

Throughout Egypt, he ordered the name of Amen to be erased from the inscriptions of the temples.

Akhenaton's reign extended seventeen years, much of it as co-regent. After he abdicated the throne, the worship of Amen was reinstated. The works of Akhenaton were destroyed. His name was deleted throughout the rest of Egyptian history. He was referred to as *'the criminal'*, and *'the rebel'*.

In order to judge his behaviour, one must ask the people of any country what their reaction would be if their leader decided that his church, of all the churches, was the only right one. Would they call him an enlightened monotheist? Furthermore, what if this leader decided to actually close all other churches, because, in his view, they were no good? Would he be called an enlightened monotheist?

The people of any country would surely react as ancient Egyptians reacted, because their leader would not be an enlightened monotheist, but a tyrannical dictator.

Akhenaton spent most of his youth in the Eastern Delta and at **Onnu**(*Heliopolis*). In the Eastern Delta area, he was influenced by Aton. Aton is the disk of the sun as a physical manifestation of Ra. At **Onnu**(*Heliopolis*), Akhenaton was educated by the priests of Ra, the ancient Egyptian solar deity.

There were very many *neteru(gods)* in Egypt. Some deities had only local distinction. Others, like Amen, Ra and **Ausar**(*Osiris*), were recognized throughout Egypt. Aton was among this multitude of deities, and it was not a new idea which was introduced by Akhenaton. Aton does appear in a few texts from the time of the Twelfth Dynasty (991 - 1783 BCE). It appeared frequently since the time of Tuthomosis IV (1401-1391 BCE).

Akhenaton exalted Aton over and above the other **neteru**. The Egyptian religion was always monotheist. The **neteru** represented the various aspects of the One Great God (see page 64 for more details).

Akhenaton's seventeen-year reign was mostly a co-regency. He reigned the first twelve years in conjunction with his father, Amenhotep III. It was very probable that the last few years of his reign was a co-regency with his brother Semenkhkare.

From the start of the co-regency, Amenhotep IV offended the Amonite priesthood by building temples to his God, the Aton, within the boundaries of the established Amen-Ra temples at Karnak. He also did not invite the traditional priests to any of the festivities. In his fifth year, he changed his name to Akhenaton, in honour of the Aton.

Because of the hostile climate which he created, Tiye, his powerful mother convinced both her son, Akhenaton, and her husband, Amenhotep III, to leave **Ta-Apet**(*Thebes*) and go to their new capital city at Tell el Amarna, 320 km (200 mi) north of **Ta-Apet**(*Thebes*). Amenhotep IV named his new city *Akhetaton* meaning *"The city of the horizon of the Aton"*. The co-regency ended when his father died, in Akhenaton's Year 12.

When Akhenaton became sole ruler after Amenhotep III died, he shut down the other temples, stopped all financial support for them and sent the priests home. These actions made a bad situation worse.

Throughout his reign, Akhenaton relied completely on the army's support for protection. The new capital city was an armed camp with parades and processions of soldiers, infantry and chariotry in their heavy gear. This military climate is depicted in the tombs of the nobles, at Tell el Amarna.

As a last resort or as a ploy, Akhenaton, in his Year 15, was forced to install his brother, Semenkhkare, as his co-regent at **Ta-Apet**(*Thebes/Luxor*). This action only delayed the final outcome.

Semenkhkare left Amarna for **Ta-Apet**(*Thebes*), where he reversed Akhenaton's hostile actions and began building a temple to Amen.

In his Year 17, Akhenaton may have been warned by his uncle, Aye, of a threat on his life. He abdicated, disappeared, and fled to Sinai, with a small group of followers.

At and about the same time, Semenkhkare died suddenly. The co-regency of Akhenaton and Semenkhkare was succeeded by the young prince, Tutankhamen.

10. *Luxor/Thebes*(Ta-Apet)

In Luxor, you feel you are experiencing the past and the present at one and the same time.

Where does the name *'Luxor'* come from? The ancient Egyptian name of this city is ***Ta-Apet***, meaning *'the fertile (multiplier) land'*. The Greeks called it *Thebes*. Homer called it *Ehebes*, which means *'the one hundred-gated city'*, because of its buildings and large gates. The city grew over the years, and after 640 CE, the Arabs, renamed it *'Luxor'*, meaning the *'City of Palaces'*.

Ta-Apet was the seat of power from 2100 to 750 BCE.

The New Kingdom Pharaohs made ***Ta-Apet***(*Thebes*) their main residence. The city had a population of nearly one million, at that time.

Ta-Apet(*Thebes*) was one of the four ancient Egyptian cosmological centres [the others are: ***Onnu***(*Heliopolis*), ***Men-Nefer***(*Memphis*) and ***Khmunu***(*Hermopolis*)]. ***Ta-Apet***'s cosmological focus was Amen, especially when Amen combines with Min, as Min-Amen, he is shown with an erect phallus, with the flail cocked over his upraised arm. Min-Amen symbolizes the creative urge manifested as the universal sexuality. In the Greek mythology, Min-Amen and his flail is equated to Zeus and his thunderbolt.

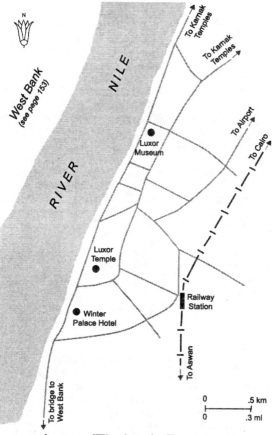

Luxor (Thebes) East Bank

East Bank

The main attractions on the east bank are the temples of Luxor and Karnak, and the Luxor Museum.

Luxor Museum

The Luxor Museum is located about halfway between the Luxor and Karnak temples. It is a small, but nicely arranged museum, featuring unique ancient Egyptian artwork, from the Middle and New Kingdoms.

The Apet and Feast of the Valley Festivals

Among the many festivals, held at *Ta-Apet(Thebes)* are the *Apet Feast* and the *Feast of the Valley*. The Apet Feast celebrated the 2 km (1.25 mi) journey of Amen from his sanctuary at Karnak Temple to the temple of Luxor and back again. The statue of Amen traveled partly on land, carried in a model boat on the shoulders of the priests, and partly in a real boat on the river, while crowds of spectators gathered on the banks. Scenes from an Apet Feast, celebrated during the reign of Tutankhamen, decorate the walls of a colonnade in the Luxor temple, and give a lively impression of the occasion.

It is ironic that the present-day Moslems of Luxor, unconsciously perform the same ancient festivities, starting at the Abu-el-Haggay mosque located at Luxor Temple.

Luxor/Thebes - East Bank

The boat of Amen [which means "The Hidden One" (invisible to all)] still tours *Ta-Apet(Thebes)*, as it always did, yet for a different reason.

Accomodations (Major Places)

Egyptian Hotel Assoc. (Tel: 348 3313 / 371 2134)
 Hilton Luxor ***** (Tel: 384 933)
 Isis ***** (Tel: 382 750)
 Jolie Ville ***** (Tel: 384 855)
 Luxor **** (Tel: 580 620)
 Sheraton ***** (Tel: 384 463)
 Akhnaten **** (Tel: 580 850)
 Etap Luxor **** (Tel: 382 011)
 Winter Palace **** (Tel: 580 422)
 Egotel *** (Tel: 384 912)
 Emilio *** (Tel: 383 570)
 Savoy *** (Tel: 580 522)
 St. Maria ** (Tel: 383 372 / 382 603)
 Windsor ** (Tel: 382 847)
 The Youth Hostel (Tel: 382 750)

Some Floating Hotels:

Isis Boat and Osiris Boat operated by Nile Hilton (Tel: 840 880).
Toth Boat and Atun Boat (Sheraton Int'l) (Tel: 348 5571, 348 8215).

How to Get To Luxor

1 - Express Trains - fully air-conditioned sleepers, and a restaurant car. The trip is about 12 hours long. (Contact: Wagons Lits. Tel: 349 2365)

2 - By Air - Egypt Air operates regular daily flights. Flying time: 45 minutes. (Contact: Egypt Air, Tel: 390-2444)

3 - By Nile Motor Vessels - Trips are organised by travel agents.

4 - By Air-conditioned Buses - Cairo-Luxor. Reservation Office, Ahmed Helmy St. (Tel: 846 658).

Luxor Temple

Luxor Temple was called by ancient Egyptians as the *Southern Harem* (sacred). It is located in the centre of town. Schwaller de Lubicz called this temple, *'Temple of Man'*, because, in his view, the design and function of its major parts is based on the creation and destiny of man.

This temple was built on the same site of a small Middle Kingdom temple. Tuthomosis III (1490-1436 BCE) built a shrine on the site. But it was Amenhotep III (1405-1367 BCE) who did the bulk of the major work, followed by Ramses II. Tutankhamen, Nectanebo, Alexander the Great, and various Romans added continuously to it.

The Main Features of the Temple include:

1 - The Avenue of the human-headed Sphinx, originally connected this temple to the Karnak Temple, for a distance of 2 km (1.25 mi). Only 200m (650ft) of these sphinxes remain, located north of the Luxor pylon. The man-headed sphinxes are those of Amenhotep III. They are exact replicas of each other.

2 - The huge pylon entrance - was built by Ramses II. It also has two seated statues of the king. They were two of the original six statues, four seated and two standing.

Originally, two large obelisks stood in front of the pylon. However, only one remains, while the other now stands in Place de la Concorde, in Paris.

Ramses II's battle of Kadesh is depicted on the exterior side of this pylon.

3 - The Court, beyond the pylon, was built by Ramses II (1304-1237 BCE), and was bordered on three sides by double rows of columns. On the northwestern side of the Court is Tuthomosis III's shrine to *Ta-pet*'s triad: Amen-Mut-Khnosu.

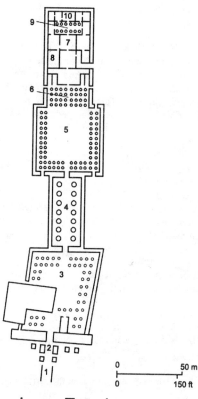

Luxor Temple

In the northeastern part of the Court is the Mosque of Abul Haggag, built on top of this Pharaonic sacred structure.

Notice the striding colossus of Ramses II in the southeast corner.

4 - The Colonnade, built by Amenhotep III, has fourteen smooth papyrus-shaped columns. The walls behind the columns were decorated during the reign of Tutankhamen (1361-1352 BCE), and they show the Apet Festival, in great detail, with the King Tutankhamen, the nobility and the common people joining the triumphal procession of Amen, Mut and Khonsu, from the Karnak Temple.

5 - The Peristyle Court of Amenhotep III, that is surrounded on three sides by double rows of pillars, with papyrus-budded capitals.

6 - The Hypostyle Hall, containing 32 pillars, connects to a room with eight columns, then to another room with four columns.

7 - The Inner Sancutary. This Holy of Holies was almost completely reconstructed by Alexander the Great, who is shown making offerings on both the inside and outside walls.

8 - The Divine (Spiritual) Marriage (See opposite page).

9 - Hall of the Twelve Columns is located past the Inner Sanctuary.

10 - Triple Sanctuary is at the farthest end of the Temple.

The Luxor Temple is open from 6am to 10pm in summer; from 7am to 9pm in winter; and from 6am to 6:30pm during Ramadan.

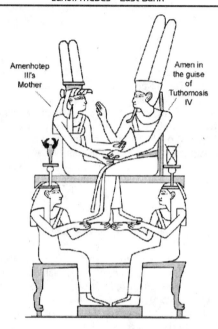

☞ The "Birth Room", to the eastern side of the chapel, contains a clear scene of the Divine (symbolically) Marriage. Amen is shown visiting Mutemuia (Amenhotep III's mother), in the 'guise' of Tuthomosis IV (Amenhotep III's father).

In ancient Egypt, divine birth was looked upon as an aspect of royal birth. Although the child was regarded spiritually as the son of the deity, this did not exclude the human father or the sexual relationship between the parents. In symbolic terms, the spirit of the deity (the Holy Spirit) used the physical body of the king to produce the child.

Temples of Karnak

The Temples of Karnak are located 2 km (1.25 mi) north of Luxor Temple. Its ancient name was *Apet-sut*, or '*The Numerator of Places*'. The design and enumeration in this temple symbolize the physical creation of the universe.

The original sanctuary of the Temple was built during the Middle Kingdom period. The oldest part of the complex is the White Pavillion, of *Sen-usert*(*Sesostris*) I (1971-1926 BCE). The rest of the temples, pylons, courts, columns and reliefs were the work of New Kingdom pharaohs.

The temple is dedicated to Amen, Mut, and Khonsu.

Since the Arab conquest, it became known as *"al-Karnak"*.

The main axis (west-east) of the temple:

1 - The Avenue of the Rams, which is a pathway, is lined with sphinxes with heads of rams, each one exactly like the next, with great precision. It was used to link the first pylon to the east bank of the Nile.

The first and largest pylon is 113m (370ft) wide, and 15m (50ft) high, and dates to King Nekhtebo of the 30th Dynasty.

2 - Great Courtyard - This courtyard includes the following features:
- On the far right, there is the Temple of Ramses III, dedicated to Amen, with its courtyard surrounded on three sides, by Ramses III (in his form as *Ausar*) pillars.
- To the left is the triple shrine of Seti II. The three small chapels held the sacred barques of Amen, Mut and Khonsu, during the lead-up to the Apet Festival.

Luxor/Thebes - East Bank

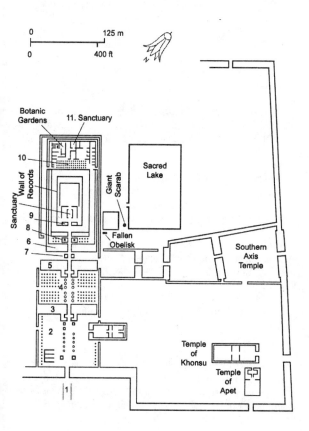

Temples of Karnak *(Partial)*

- In the middle of the Court, are the remains of a double colonnade, built by King Taharqa (690-664 BCE).
- A portico of strong columns with closed papyrus capitals, is on the left side. Next to them is a row of ram-headed sphinxes, by Ramses II.

3 - The Second Pylon was built by Horemheb (1348-1335 BCE). Ramses II raised two colossal pink granite statues of himself on both sides of the entrance.

4 - The Great Hypostyle Hall - is one of the world's greatest architectural masterpieces. It is 102m x 53m (335ft x 174ft). It began with ***Amenhotep***(*Amenophis*) III, and continued with Seti I and finished by Ramses II. It has 134 columns, 24m (79ft) high. The columns' circumference is 10m (33ft), and at the top of the open papyrus-shaped capital is 15m (50ft). All columns and walls are fully inscripted and decorated. The outer walls of this Hall are decorated with some of the war records of Seti I (1333-1304 BCE) and Ramses II.

5 - The Third Pylon was built by Amenhotep III.

6 - The Fourth Pylon was built by Tuthomosis I.

7 - Narrow Court. Between the Third and Fourth Pylons, is a narrow court. Tuthomosis I (1528-1510 BCE) raised two obelisks in front of the Fourth Pylon. Only one is still standing. The obelisk of Tuthomosis I, is 22m (70ft) high, and 143 tons in weight.

8 - The Fifth Pylon was constructed by Tuthomosis I. In front of this pylon, Hatshepsut (1490-1468 BCE) raised two obelisks. Only one is standing. The Hatshepsut Obelisk is 30m (98ft) in height, and weighs 320 tons. Tuthomosis III built a 25m (82ft) high sandstone structure around Hatshepsut's obelisk. Hatshepsut's other obelisk lies broken, near the Sacred Lake of the Karnak Temple.

9 - The Sixth Pylon - now in a ruined state, was built by Tuthomosis III. It leads to the sacred barque sanctuary, and long lists of Tuthomosis III's records are depicted on surrounding walls.

The present sanctuary was built by the brother of Alexander the Great, Philip Arrhidaeus (323-316 BCE), on the location of an earlier one, built by Tuthomosis III, which in turn replaced the original Middle Kingdom Sanctuary.

10 - Hall of Ceremonies - *Akh-Menu* is located past the central court, which dates back to the Middle Kingdom, and which leads to a large Hall of Ceremonies, built by Tuthomosis III. This unique Festival Hall was built in commemoration of Tuthomosis III's completion of the Heb-Sed tradition.

11 - Last Sanctuary (Holy of Holies) is located beyond the Festival Hall.

One of the three rooms that form this sanctuary, contains what is called "**The Botanical Garden**". The room walls are carved with plants and animals that Tuthomosis III brought back from his wars in Asia.

Karnak's Southern Axis

The southern axis begins between the Third and the Fourth Pylons, of the main west-east axis. It has a small hypostyle hall, several pylons, and a ruined sanctuary. The temple was started by Ramses III, and was added to by other pharaohs.

Other Points of Interest:

(Location map on page 147)

1 - Temple of Khonsu - in a fairly good state of repair. It has a small hypostyle hall and a ruined sanctuary. The temple was started by Ramses III, and added to by other pharaohs.

2 - Temple of Apet - dedicated to the hippopotamus-*netert*(*goddess*) Apet. A 2 km (1.25 mi) long avenue of human-headed sphinxes connected the Temple of Apet to the Luxor Temple.

3 - Pavilion of *Sen-usert*(*Sesostris*) I - This is the oldest structure in the Karnak Complex. Sen-usert I (1971-1926 BCE) built this very harmonious architectural gem. It contains plenty of geodesic information, such as all the provinces of Egypt with each's respective surface area, as well as the Nile normal flood elevations at three main points, along the river.

☞ Visiting the area that includes the Pavilion requires a special ticket from the kiosk outside the Karnak Temple. Therefore, make sure you purchase this special ticket, along with your main ticket, before you enter the temple.

4 - The Sacred Lake - was used for purification ceremonies of the priests. It drew its water from the Nile. The lake was 120m x 77m (400ft x 250ft), and was surrounded by buildings, storehouses, aviary, and housing for the priests.

There is also a large statue of a scarab, dating to King

Amenhotep III, next to the Sacred Lake.

5 - The Fallen Obelisk - The top portion of Hatshepsut's fallen obelisk is lying on the ground, near the Sacred Lake. If one hits the obelisk with a hand, the entire enormous block resonates like a tuning fork, which can be detected by putting your ear at the angle of the top pyramidion. This phenomenon is certainly an instinctive property of granite when cut to an obelisk shape.

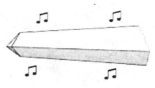

6 - Sound & Light Show - Three or four Sound & Light Shows are performed every evening at the Karnak Temple, in different languages. Visitors walk through the temple, to some stadium-type seating arranged behind the Sacred Lake, where they can enjoy the rest of the narration. Through the use of words, light, and music, the narrator tells the story of this magnificent temple.

Entrance fee is EP30 plus EP3 sales tax. Private shows are available with prior arrangement, for 50 people or more.

Winter	*6:00pm*	*7:15pm*	*8:30pm*	*9:45pm*
Summer	*7:45pm*	*9:00pm*	*10:15pm*	*11:30pm*
Mon.	English	French	Spanish	
Tues.	German	Japanese	English	
Wed.	German	English	French	
Thur.	English	French	Arabic	
Fri.	Italian	English	French	Spanish
Sat.	French	Japanese	English	German
Sun.	German	English	French	Italian

West Bank

Except during the reign of Akhenaton, Egyptians buried their dead on the west bank of the Nile. The west is where the sun sets, i.e. the end of the daytime. The symbolism, typical of ancient Egyptians, is simple, and therefore, powerful.

The West Bank of Luxor(Ta-Apet) also contains temples that commemorate the major achievements of the different kings did, during their earthly existence.

The main attractions in the West Bank include:

1 - Valley of the Kings

2 - Valley of the Queens

3 - Commemorative (popularly but wrongly known as "Mortuary") Temples of

- Hatshepsut (Deir el Bahari)
- Ramesseum (Ramses II)
- Seti I
- Ramses III (Medinat Habu)
- Colossi of Memnon (the Vanished Temple of Amenhotep III)

4 - Tombs of the Nobles

5 - Village of Workmen (Deir el Medina)

Luxor/Thebes - West Bank

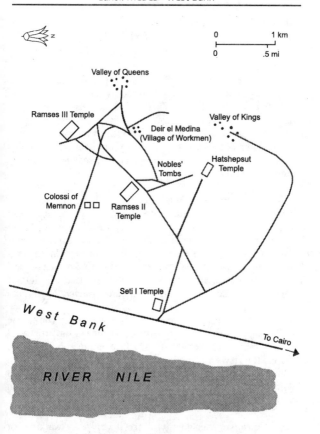

Luxor - West Bank Site Plan

1 - Valley of the Kings
(Location map on page 153)

Tuthomosis I was the first pharaoh to have his tomb cut, around 1495 BCE, and was followed by later kings, over the next five hundred years. There are 62 tombs in the valley. Each tomb is numbered in order of its discovery, but only about a dozen tombs are currently open to the public.

Tutankhamen's tomb is the only one that still includes the mummy. The rest of the mummies are scattered in museums all over the world.

The royal tombs generally consist of a long, inclined rock-hewn corridor descending into either an antechamber or a series of sometimes pillared halls, and ending in the burial chamber. The walls of the tombs are decorated almost exclusively with the afterlife transformation process from the carnal to the purly spiritual (resurrection) to rejoin the source.

The colourful paintings and reliefs are extracts from their Sacred Texts. (see Chapter: *Understanding Ancient Egyptians*)

The visitor has time to visit only 3-4 tombs. The theme in the tombs, tends to be repetitive. However, the artistry of these tombs, over the 500 years, will be more appreciated, if the visitor views a sampling of tombs from different periods. Select one tomb of each period, and as most people do, you will probably visit the small and unimpressive Tutankhamen tomb, just because of its fame.

☞ Conserve your energy. Take it very easy walking, or climbing the stairs. Drink plenty of water before and after each tomb, to avoid having dehydration sneak up on you. Remember to bring along a flashlight (torch).

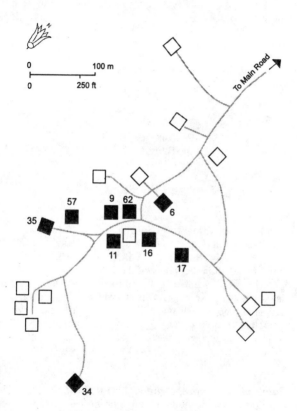

Valley of the Kings
(Showing Tomb Numbers)

Below, is a list of the major tombs, which can be seen in the Valley of the Kings: *(Location map on page 155)*

```
Tomb No:  34 - Tuthomosis III
          35 - Amenhotep(Amenophis) II
          62 - Tutankhamen
          57 - Horemheb
          16 - Ramses I
          17 - Seti I
          11 - Ramses III
           9 - Ramses VI
           6 - Ramses IX
```

Tombs of the Early Period
(Early 18th Dynasty)

Tomb of Tuthomosis III (No 34)

This is a very hard to reach tomb.

Tuthomosis III (1490-1436 BCE) was one of the first to build his tomb in the Valley of the Kings.

The burial chamber is shaped like a cartouche. The roof is supported by two pillars, between which is the king's empty, red sandstone sarcophagus. The walls are decorated with a complete version of the <u>Book of What is in the Duat</u>. The sequence of passages of the book follow around the wall clockwise.

Tomb of Amenhotep(Amenophis) II (No 35)

One of the deepest structures in the valley, Amenhotep II's (1436-1413 BCE) tomb has more than 90 steps.

The walls are decorated with the complete version of the <u>Book of What is in the Duat</u>, with a yellow background, to appear as if it were a papyrus scroll.

Luxor/Thebes - West Bank 157

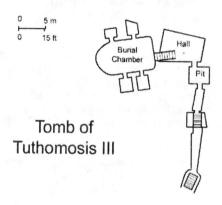

Tomb of Tuthomosis III

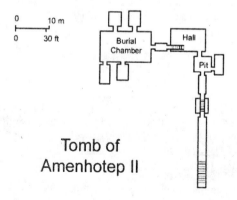

Tomb of Amenhotep II

Tombs of the Middle Period
(Early 19th Dynasty)

Tomb of Ramses I (No 16)
It has the shortest entrance corridor in the valley. It has a single almost square burial chamber, containing the king's pink granite sarcophagus. Ramses I (1335-1333 BCE) died suddenly. The chamber is the only part of the tomb that is nicely decorated. It is interesting to note the different phases of the work, in the uncompleted corridor.

Tomb of Seti I (No 17)
Seti I (1333-1304 BCE)'s tomb is the most preserved tomb in the valley. It contains the Litany of Ra portions of the books: What is in the Duat, and the Book of the Gates.

It drops over 100m (330ft). The long corridor ends with the burial chamber. Its first section is a pillared hall decorated with texts from the Book of the Gates. The burial chamber originally contained Seti's alabaster sarcophagus, but that is now in the Soane Museum in London.

Tombs of the Late Period
(Late 20th Dynasty)

Tomb of Ramses VI (No 9)
The tomb is 80m (260ft) long. The passageway is decorated with the complete texts of the Book of the Caverns, and The Book of What is in the Duat, as well as portions of The Book of Day and Night, and The Book of Aker.

Tomb of Ramses IX (No 6)
It is similar in content and style to the Tomb of Ramses VI. Likewise, the *netert*(*goddess*) Nut is the feature of the ceiling painting, surrounded by sacred barques full of stars.

Luxor/Thebes - West Bank

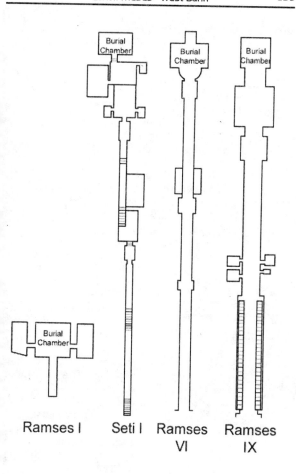

Ramses I   Seti I   Ramses VI   Ramses IX

Tomb of Tutankhamen (No 62)

(Location map on page 155)

On 4 November 1922, the tomb of Tutankhamen (1361-1352 BCE) was discovered in the Valley of the Kings, by Howard Carter.

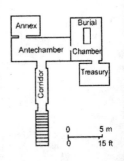

Carter struggled for six seasons, searching the area, because he was convinced the tomb was nearby.

Tutankhamen's tomb is small and for the most part undecorated. Only the small burial chamber is decorated with texts from the Book of Coming Forth by Day (Book of the Dead). The walls here, are covered with fresh-looking paintings, showing the ascension and subsequent reception of Tutankhamen in the afterlife.

Only the gold-plated inner-mummy case, with the body of Tut still within it, are on site. The rest of the treasures of the tomb (the second coffin of gilded wood, the solid gold mummy case and the magnificent funerary mask), and other artifacts from the other chambers of the tomb, are all in the Egyptian Museum in Cairo.

2 - Valley of the Queens

(Location map on page 153)

This valley contains the tombs of queens and family members, of the 19th and 20th Dynasties. Of the 25 tombs in the Valley of the Queens, only a handful were completed and decorated. Three tombs are of interest:

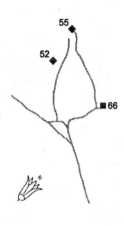

1 - The Tomb of Nefertari (No 66)

The lines and colours of this decorated tomb are supurb. It belongs to Nefertari, the wife of Ramses II (1304-1237 BCE).

2 - The Tomb of Amen-Hir-Khopsef (No 55)

Amen-Hir-Khopsee was the son of Ramses III, and was nine years old when he died. The scenes on the tomb walls depict his father introducing him to the different deities, then leaving him at the threshold of the beyond. Then the child goes alone, through the transformation process.

A five month old mummified fetus was buried next to Amen-Hir-Khopsef.

3 - The Tomb of Queen Titi (No 52)

Queen Titi was wife and consort to one of the Ramses. She has a small but nicely decorated tomb.

3 - Commemorative Temples

Hatshepsut Commemorative Temple *(Deir el Bahri)*
(Location map on page 153)

Hatshepsut ruled from 1490 to 1468 BCE, and did not engage Egypt in any war.

Her temple is very similar to an earlier temple, that was built 600 years earlier, by the Mentu-hoteps, the kings of the Ninth Dynasty. The ruins of the earlier temple are located to the south, next to Hatshepsut's Temple.

Hatshepsut's Commemorative Temple consists of:

1 - A **causeway**, 36m (120ft) wide, that leads onto the three huge terraced courts.

2 - The **lower terrace** consists of a double colonnade, formed of two rows of eleven columns, on each side of the ramp. The walls around the colonnades feature scenes of bird-catching with nets, and the transport of a pair of obelisks.

3 - The **central terrace** contains:
• Double colonnades of 11 columns on the right side. The walls there depict the "Divine Birth" of Hatshepsut.
• Double colonnades of 11 columns on the left side. The walls there depict the naval expedition, that she dispatched, to the legendary land of Punt.
• On the far right, there is the ***Anpu****(Anubis)* Shrine, with colourful reliefs.
• On the far left is the chapel of ***Het-Heru****(Hathor)*, which contains 14 ***Het-Heru****(Hathor)*-headed columns. This leads into successive rock-hewn rooms, which lead to the shrine. The walls throughout have fine, colourful reliefs.

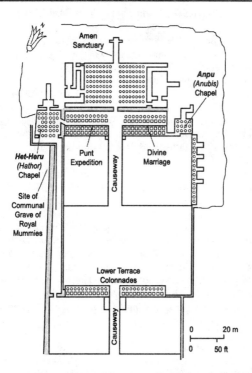

Temple of Hatshepsut

4 - The third terrace is in a ruined state. It was here that the early Christians settled, and made this temple their monastery, defacing and destroying the ancient sacred inscriptions. Amen sanctuary is located at the end of the temple. This sanctuary is hewn out of the cliff.

The Hatshepsut/Tuthomosis III - The Real Story

Many people like to view the Hatshepsut/Tuthomosis III story as a contest of man against woman. In order to understand the episode of Hatshepsut and Tuthomosis III, we must start with his father, Tuthomosis II.

Tuthomosis II (c. 1510-1490 BCE) was born of a minor wife, and not the Great Royal Wife. In order to inherit the throne, he married his half-sister, Hatshepsut, the heiress daughter of his father and Queen Ahmose (the Great Royal Wife).
Tuthomosis II had a son, Tuthomosis III, by a concubine named Isis. Tuthomosis II also had a daughter, Neferure from Hatshepsut. Tuthomosis II died shortly thereafter.

Since the line of the throne inheritance went through the eldest daughter, the normal method for Tuthomosis III to inherit the throne, was for him to marry Neferure, who was the legal heiress. The marriage did not occur, possibly because of Hatshepsut's refusal to consent. Hatshepsut continued to insist that Neferure was the legal heiress, *'Lady of the Two Lands, Mistress of Upper and Lower Egypt'*. But Neferure did not rule. Instead, her mother illegally took over.

Tuthomosis III was only five years old when his father died. Because of his young age, Queen Hatshepsut appointed herself as his guardian. Two years later, Hatshepsut began sharing kingship with Tuthomosis III, and dressed as a man. Tuthomosis III had recently received the approval of the priesthood, so as to get himself "adopted" by Amen, in order to ensure his right to the throne. Tuthomosis III was kept powerless until Year 16 of the co-regency, when Neferure, the legal heiress died.
After Neferure's death, Tuthomosis III gained increasing

importance.

When Hatshepsut died, after 22 years of the co-regency, Tuthomosis III became the sole ruler of Egypt.

Tuthomosis III defaced some (but not all) of Hatshepsut's monuments. Did he really avenge what she did to him? Upon rational thinking of the subject of monument appropriation (See Chapter 7 - *Understanding Ancient Egyptians*), the answer is possibly *yes*, but without jeopardising her divine responsibilities. The result was selective defacement in certain situations. Not until we understand the ancient Egyptians' deep religious beliefs, will we be able to understand such selectivity.

Did Hatshepsut and/or Neferure refuse Tuthomosis III, as husband for Neferure? Why didn't Hatshepsut let the legal heiress, her daughter Neferure, govern? Was Tuthomosis III refused because of Hatshepsut's ambitions or was he paying the price for his father's personal deeds, or was it just a typical family feud? We have no knowledge of the answers to these questions. However, we know that ancient Egyptian women achieved the highest regard in society, throughout history.

Communal Grave of Royal Mummies on this Site

In 1876, a huge shaft in the immediate vicinity of Hatshepsut Commemorative Temple was found. It contained the mummies of 40 pharaohs, queens and nobles, such as: Amenhotep I, Tuthomosis II and III, Seti I and Ramses I and III.

Because the tomb robbers did not allow their kings to rest in peace, the priests started transporting the mummies from one place to another, and then finally moved them to this communal grave.

The Ramesseum Commemorative Temple
(Location map on page 153)

Ramses II (1304-1237 BCE) built this temple. The main features of this [now ruined] temple include:

1 - The huge 1st and 2nd pylons, which feature reliefs of Ramses' military campaign in Kadesh, Syria.

2 - The Great Court includes the double colonnades (in a ruined state). Near the western stairs, is part of the Colossus of Ramses II. When it stood, it was 18m (60ft), with his crown it was 23m (75ft) high. It is said that the Persian King Cambyses destroyed it, about 526 BCE. Others say that it was the result of an earthquake in 27 BCE.

3 - The Great Hypostyle Hall has 29, of the original 48 columns, still standing. The ceiling here features astronomical scenes, and provides information on the Egyptian calendrical system.
The hall contains three naves, in which the outer columns are fitted with bud capitals and the inner with opened papyrus capitals.

4 - Sanctuaries and surrounding rooms are now in a ruined state.

Commemorative Temple of Seti I
(Location map on page 153)

Even though only about one-third of the original structure of Seti I (1333-1304 BCE) still stands, it is worth a visit. The wall reliefs are the best in the New Kingdom.

A section of the temple that was begun by Seti I, was completed in a lesser quality fashion, by Ramses II.

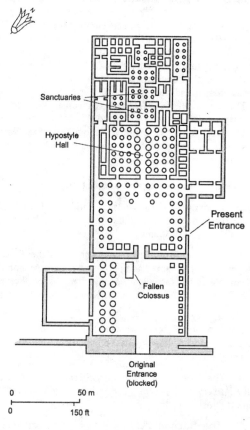

Ramesseum Commemorative Temple

Ramses III Commemorative Temple (Medinat Habu)
(Location map on page 153)

The work on this site was begun by Amenhotep I (1550-1528 BCE), and was added to by Hatshepsut, Tuthmosis III, and other rulers, right through to the Ptolemies. Ramses III, however, constructed the main buildings of the complex.

This temple complex is second only to the Temples of Karnak in size and complexity.

The name, *Medinat Habu*, was given to the temple, by the early Christians, who inhabited this sacred site.

The wall reliefs here are enormous, yet lack elegance. The reliefs, however, are neatly cut, as much as 20 cm (8 in) deep into the walls.

The main features of this complex include:

1 - Pavilion - it is an unusual building. It looks like a militaristic fort, and the decoration on the walls are mostly devoted to military themes.

2 - The Original Temple - (known as the Temple of Hatshepsut). This small temple was built by Amenhotep I, and completed by Hatshepsut. Many pharaohs left their marks here: Tuthmosis III, Akhenaton, Horemheb, Seti I, and the Ptolemies.

3 - The First Pylon - is covered on both sides with representations and inscriptions of Ramses III's victory over the Syrians.

4 - The First Court - contains columns with Ramses III in the *Ausar(Osiris)* form. The reliefs in this area show the king's victory over the Libyans.

5 - The Second Pylon - shows inscriptions detailing Ramses III's victory over the *"Peoples of the Sea"*. More about these people, under item 8 below.

Luxor/Thebes - West Bank

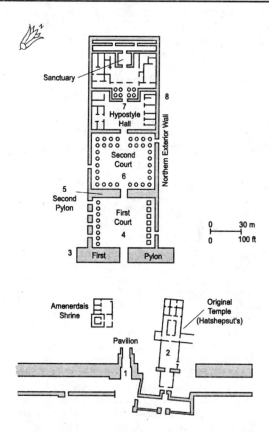

Ramses III Temple

6 - The Second Court - has very interesting wall reliefs behind the colonnades. The walls depict Festivals of Min and Ptah-Sokar, as well as military themes where the king presents the prisoners, and parts of their bodies, to the **neteru**(*gods*), which indicate some deep, but unknown to us, metaphysical meanings. The walls also show scenes related to the creation mysteries.

7 - The Third Court, Offices, and Sanctuaries. This area was originally roofed over. The walls include beautiful reliefs of various objects: musical instruments, jewelry, and other artifacts.

8 - The Northern Exterior Wall depicts the naval battle against the "Peoples of the Sea".

The "Peoples of the Sea" began their mass invasion of the coastal plain of Canaan (present-day Israel, Palestine, and Lebanon), around 1174 BCE, which coincided with the Greek war against Troy. The temple walls here depict the fact that the invading people were after permanent settlement, for they consisted of whole families. The wall inscriptions also indicate that the "Peoples of the Sea" were a combination of Peleset (which are Philistines - the word Palestine came from Peleset), Tjekker, Shekelsh, Danu and Weshesh. Ramses III defeated the invaders in a naval battle, and many of the captives were allowed to settle in southwest Canaan.

After the reign of Ramses III, Egypt lost control over Palestine and the Philistines established themselves in the coastal plains of Canaan and started expanding towards the Dead Sea and the River Jordan. It was at the same time that the Israelites were trying to establish themselves in this area, after they left Egypt. Because of the power vacuum left after the reign of Ramses III, both Philistines and Israelites began fighting, and thus emerged the biblical stories of Saul, David and Goliath.

Colossi of Memnon & The Vanished Temple

(Location map:on page 153)

The two 20m (65ft) high colossi of the faceless, seated statues of **Amenhotep**(*Amenophis*) III (1405-1367 BCE), are all that remains of a splendid temple.

It is incredible to think that there was a temple here, when you can't find a single block left.

However, a temple existed, which is described on a stele, now in the Egyptian Museum, as being built from *"white sandstone, with gold throughout, a floor covered with silver, and doors covered with electrum"*.

In 27 BCE, a major earthquake occured, that damaged this and many other monuments in **Ta-Apet**(*Thebes*). As a result, the statues suffered cracks, and were said to sing. At daybreak, every morning, the statues gave out a prolonged and harmonious sound. Greek poets soon after created their legend around this strange sound, and great Greek and Roman historians testified to the "stone that sings".

The Greeks named the two statues after Memnon, the legendary hero killed at the Trojan Wars, who, each morning, called his mother Eos, the Dawn goddess, and she bewailed him, shedding tears that were the dewdrops.

4 - Tombs of the Nobles
(Location map on page 153)

There are at least 400 tombs which date from the 6th dynasty to the Greco-Roman period, in this area. But only about seven tombs are worth visiting. As at Saqqara, the thematic material is mainly drawn from daily life activities, all of which have a deeper symbolic and metaphysical significance.

The most important tombs of the area are:

Tomb of Nakht (No 52)
Nakht was a Scribe of Granaries. His tomb shows scenes of plowing, sowing and preparing grain, hunting, fishing and feasting. The most popular scene of the three musicians, that you now see on T-shirts, posters, postcards and papyrus paintings, is depicted in this tomb.

Tomb of Menna (No 69)
This tomb provides one of the most complete records of harvests, feasts, and related activities.

Tomb of Ramose (No 55)
Ramose was the vizier, during the reigns of Amenhotep III and Akhenaton.

This tomb was never actually finished because Ramose followed Akhenaton to his new city at Tell el Amarna. There are many beautiful scenes here. Among them is the famous scene of the wailing women.

Tomb of Khaemhet (No 57)
Khaemhet was *Amenhotep(Amenophis)* III's overseer of the granaries.

Tomb of Sennofer (No 96)
Sennofer was *Amenhotep(Amenophis)* II's overseer of the gardens. The ceiling of this tomb is covered with clear paint-

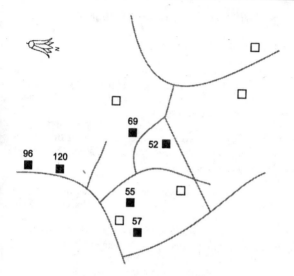

Tombs of the Nobles

ings of grapes and vines.

Tomb of Rekhmire (No 120)

Rekhmire was the vizier of both Tuthomosis III and *Amenhotep* II. This tomb is one of the best preserved in the area. Its features show a detailed catalogue of real life activities. This tomb has provided scholars with a wealth of information on Egyptian law, taxes, and other civil matters, as well as insights into crafts and industries. Rekhmire is also shown receiving tributes from foreign lands.

5 - Village of Workmen (Deir el Medina)
(Location map on page 153)

The points of attractions in this area are:

1 - The ruins of the village, built at the time of Amenhotep I (1550-1528 BCE), and inhabited by the people who worked in the building and decorating of the tombs and temples, over a 500-year span.

The village has been unearthed to find well-planned roads and more than 100 two-storey houses, made of dried brick. Several personal findings have told us a lot about these people and their daily lives.

Their tombs were located on the west side of the village, each consisted of a chapel and small painted basement. Some of them are breathtaking, such as:

The Tomb of Sennedjem (No 1) was a 19th Dynasty servant in the so-called *Place of Truth*. The tomb has one small, oval chamber, with magnificent wall paintings.

Other tombs worth seeing are Ipuy and Inherkha.

2 - The Temple of Ptolemy IV Philopator (222-205 BCE), which was occupied by early Christians, who gave it a local name, *"deir el medina"*, meaning *'monastary of the town'*. The plan for the original temple may have been set by Amenhotep, son of Hapu, in the 18th Dynasty. The present structure is entirely Ptolemaic, and was built by the Ptolemy IV Philopator (222 - 205 BCE).

The temple is dedicated to **Het-Heru**(*Hathor*), the *netert*(*goddess*) of pleasure and love, and to Maat, the *netert*(*goddess*) of truth and the personification of cosmic order.

The back of the temple shows reliefs of the most complete and beautiful scene of the Weighing of the Heart process during the Judgment Day.

Ancient Egyptians expressed their metaphysical beliefs in a story form, like a sacred drama or a *mystery play*. The following are the Egyptians' symbolic representations of the process of the Judgment Day *Mystery Play*.

a.) The soul of the deceased is led to the Hall of Judgment of the Double-Maat. Maat's symbol is the ostrich feather. Her feather is customarily mounted on the scales.

b.) *Anpu(Anubis)*, as opener of the way, guides the soul to the scales and weighs the heart (as a metaphor for conscience), against the feather of truth.

c.) The seated *Ausar(Osiris)* presides in the Hall of Justice. The jury consists of forty-two judges. Each judge has jurisdiction over a specific sin or fault.

d.) The spirit of the deceased denies committing each sin/fault before its assigned judge, by reciting the forty-two Negative Confessions, that come from <u>The Book of the Coming Forth by Day</u> (commonly known as *The Book of the Dead*).

1 - Maat in her double form
2 - *Anpu (Anubis)*
3 - *Amam (Ammit)*
4 - *Tehuti (Thoth)*
5 - The deceased
6 - *Heru (Horus)*
7 - *Ausar (Osiris)*

e.) The ibis-headed **Tehuti**(*Thoth*), records the verdict, as **Anpu**(*Anubis*) weighs the heart against the feather of truth.

As a result of the weighing:
• If the pans are not balanced, it means that this person lived simply, as matter. As a result, **Amam**(*Ammit*), representing the world of pure materialism, would eat the heart.

The imperfected soul will be reborn again (reincarnated) in a new physical vehicle (body), in order to provide the soul an opportunity for further development on earth.

• If the two pans are perfectly balanced, **Ausar**(*Osiris*) gives favourable judgment: *Let the deceased depart victorious*. The perfected soul will go through the process of transformation and the subsequent rebirth, and as the Egyptian writing describes it, *becomes a star of gold and joins the company of Ra, and sails with him across the sky in his boat of millions of years.*

The 42 Negative Confessions

1. *I have not done iniquity.*
2. *I have not robbed with violence.*
3. *I have not stolen.*
4. *I have done no murder, I have done no harm.*
5. *I have not defrauded offerings.*
6. *I have not diminished obligations.*
7. *I have not plundered the **neteru**(gods).*
8. *I have not spoken lies.*
9. *I have not uttered evil words.*
10. *I have not caused pain.*
11. *I have not committed fornication.*
12. *I have caused no shedding of tears.*
13. *I have not dealt deceitfully.*

14. I have not transgressed.
15. I have not acted guilefully.
16. I have not laid waste the ploughed land.
17. I have not been an eavesdropper.
18. I have not set my lips in motion (against any man).
19. I have not been angry and wrathful, except for a just cause.
20. I have not defiled the wife of any man.
21. I have not been a man of anger.
22. I have not polluted myself.
23. I have not caused terror.
24. I have not burned with rage.
25. I have not stopped my ears against the words of Right and Truth. (Maat)
26. I have not worked grief.
27. I have not acted with insolence.
28. I have not stirred up strife.
29. I have not judged hastily.
30. I have not sought for distinctions.
31. I have not multiplied words exceedingly.
32. I have not done harm nor ill.
33. I have not cursed the King. (i.e. violation of laws).
34. I have not fouled the water.
35. I have not spoken scornfully.
36. I have not cursed the **neteru**(gods).
37. I have not made haughty my voice.
38. I have not defrauded the offerings of the **neteru**(gods).
39. I have not plundered the offerings of the blessed dead.
40. I have not filched the food of the infant.
41. I have not sinned against the **neter**(god) of my native town.
42. I have not slaughtered with evil intent the cattle of the **neter**(god).

11. Sites North of Luxor/(Ta-Apet)

The following two sites, of Dendara(Enet-ta-ntr) and Abydos(Abtu), are within a day's trip from Luxor. The distance between Dendara and Abydos is 90 km (60 mi).

Dendara(Enet-ta-ntr)

Dendara(Enet-ta-ntr) is located about 50 km (30 mi) north of Luxor. *Enet-ta-ntr* is the ancient Egyptian name for Dendara. Dendara's main Temple of *Het-Heru(Hathor)* was called *"Pr Het-Heru"* meaning *"House of Het-Heru"*. It was a major healing centre for people from all over.

The temple complex, as it stands today, was built on the site of an older temple, and is a replica of the original. The present building was first initiated by Ptolemy III, with numerous additions by subsequent Ptolemaic and Roman rulers.

The inscription on the present temple, states that the original building was erected in the far pre-Dynastic times, by "the followers of *Heru(Horus)*". Archaeological evidence shows that *Khufu* (the builder of the Great Pyramid) built a temple, presumably on this temple site. During the reign of Pepi I (2289-2255 BCE), the *Enet-ta-ntr* Temple was rebuilt. Several subsequent pharaohs left their marks in this important site.

Sites North of Luxor - Dendara

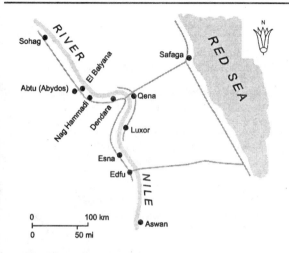

Major Festivities at the Temple of Het-Heru(*Hathor*)

1) The effigy of **Het-Heru** [meaning the house/wife of **Heru**(*Horus*)], would embark each New Year south, towards Edfu. The effigy of **Heru**(*Horus*) would leave Edfu and head northward. Both would meet at the halfway point, between Dendara and Edfu. Jointly, they journeyed to Edfu Temple.

2) In Dendara, a festival commemorating the birth of **Heru,** used to be celebrated as "*The Day of the Child in his Cradle*". It occurred at the end of the Egyptian year, and very much resembled the later Christian festival of Christmas.

3) The Egyptian New Year was celebrated here with sistrums (musical rattles), similar to our modern New Year's Day noise-making celebrations.

Dendara(*Enet-ta-ntr*) Site Main Features

1 - Het-Heru(Hathor) Main Temple
The main features of this beautiful temple include:

a. **The temple facade** with six *Het-Heru*-headed sistrum columns and a huge corniche.

b. **The Great Hypostyle Hall** with 18 similar *Het-Heru*-headed columns. The ceiling has a very interesting astronomical decoration with a representation of the twelve signs of the zodiac.

c. **The Small Hypostyle Hall** with six *Het-Heru*-headed columns. This and several surrounding rooms are fully decorated with interesting scenes.

d. **The Decorated Sanctuary** and surrounding rooms.

e. **The Roof Chapels and Sanctuaries** which are fully decorated. A part of its ceiling is carved with the famous circular Dendara zodiac. Actually, the present zodiac is a plaster cast of the original, which is now in the Louvre.

2 - Mammisi(The Birth Houses)
There are two Mammisi, from two different periods. The reliefs on the walls of both birth houses, built by Nectanebo and Nero, depict the "Divine Birth" (similar to Luxor and Hatshepsut Temples), and the infancy period of ***Heru****(Horus)*.

3 - Exterior Facade
It contains a famous painting of Queen Cleopatra, and Caesaron, her son from Julius Caesar.

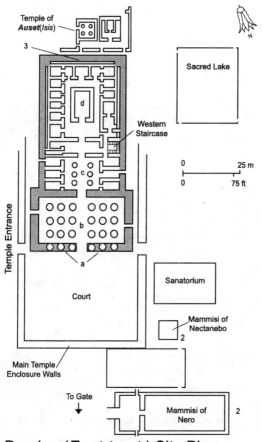

Dendara (*Enet-ta-ntr*) Site Plan

Abydos(**Abtu**)

*The ancient Egyptian **Abtu**(Abydos in Greek) is 140 km (90 mi) north of Luxor. The main features here are the two temples of Seti I and Ramses II, as well as the Ausarion (Tomb of **Ausar**).*

Ausar Temple of Seti I

This is one of Egypt's most complete temples. Relief carving during Seti's reign (1306-1290 BCE), is the best of the New Kingdom. Every centimeter of the temple walls are covered with perfectly executed scenes.

The Seti Temple was begun by Seti I, and was completed in a lesser quality, during the reign of his son, Ramses II.

Points of Main Interest

1. The Temple begins at the top of forty-two steps, representing the forty-two assessors of the Duat, where *Ausar(Osiris)* presides in the final judgment day.

2. The temple is L-shaped, and instead of being dedicated to just one principal *neter* (and that *neter*'s consort and son), it has seven sanctuaries. They are for Ptah, Ra-Horachty, Amen, as well as the Ausarion Triad (*Ausar*, *Auset*, and *Heru*) and the seventh sanctuary is for Seti I.

3. The *Ausar(Osiris)* Chapel has an overview of the various forms and functions of *Ausar(Osiris)* as symbolized by different headdresses, emblems and gestures.

4. The walls of this Temple do not show any part of the *Ausar(Osiris)* Legend that reached us through early Greek and Roman historians, or even a different *Ausar* Legend.

5. The Gallery of the Kings, contains a list of 76 cartouches of Egypt's pharaohs, from *Mena(Menes)* up to Seti I.

Sites North of Luxor - Abydos

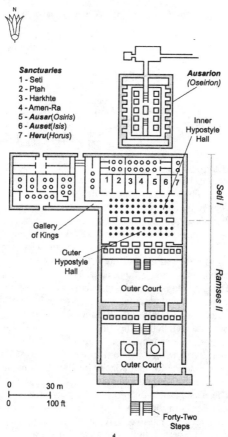

Temple at *Àbtu*(Abydos)

The Ausarion(*Oseirion*) (Tomb of Ausar)

(Location map on page 183)

The Ausarion consists of huge red granite pillars, each weighing about 100 tons. The outer walls are built of red sandstone.

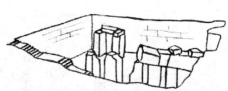

The ancient Egyptians themselves, called this place the "Tomb of *Ausar*", which academic Egyptologists, as usual, ignored, and renamed for their convenience.

The *Ausarion*(*Oseirion*) building is very similar to the Valley Temple of *Khafra*(*Chephren*), south of the Sphinx at Giza. Both have the same massive simplicity, the mighty square granite pillars and the total absence of inscriptions and carvings.

The *Ausarion* structure is partially submerged underneath the present groundwater table. The present level of the water table has risen some 6m (20ft) since New Kingdom times.

Because Seti I inscribed his name on some parts of the building, some academians were quick to attribute the building of the *Ausarion*(*Oseirion*) to Seti I. It was, however, a common practice for pharaohs to inscribe their names on others' temples and monuments.

The *Ausarion*(*Oseirion*) is extremely different from any other building in the New Kingdom. There is a huge difference between its massive, bare, and brutal simplicity as compared to the elegant and sophisticated main temple of Seti I. The *Ausarion* constitutes extreme contrast in architecture, style and design to Seti's temple.

The tremendous difference in elevation between the *Ausarion* and Seti's Temple, as well as the dramatic difference in style between the two, suggested to many scholars that the *Ausarion* is a much older building.

The evidence at the *Ausarion*, and other funerary remains at *Abtu(Abydos)*, is consistent with the evidence at Giza and elsewhere, regarding the antiquity of the Egyptian civilization, which is much older than academians are willing to admit.

Ausar Temple of Ramses II

Ramses II built another temple dedicated to *Ausar*, just northwest of Seti I's temple. The roof of this temple has collapsed. The walls still stand, and display interesting reliefs.

Abtu(Abydos), The Pilgrimage Place

Abtu(Abydos) was the major place for the worship of *Ausar(Osiris)*. Both *Abtu(Abydos)* and Saqqara were the major funerary sites from the earliest dynasties on record, and even earlier. The funerary remains at *Abtu(Abydos)* have provided scholars with much of what is known of those remote pre-Dynastic times.

As a consequence of the murder and dismemberment of *Ausar(Osiris)*, various Egyptian cities claimed the honour of being the burial place of parts of his body. *Abtu(Abydos)* claimed to be the burial place of the head of *Ausar(Osiris)*, and as such became the well-known place of pilgrimage in honour of *Ausar(Osiris)*.

The ancient Egyptian name of this place, *Abtu*, means "*the mound*" of the *Ausar(Osiris)* Head Emblem.

12. Valley of the Upper Nile

*The 200 km (124 mi) stretch between Luxor(**Ta-Apet**) and Aswan(**Sunt**) is referred to as the Valley of the Upper Nile. Major points of interest are: Esna, Nekheb(El Kab), Nekhen(Kom el Ahmer), Edfu, and Kom Ombo.*

Esna

(Location map on page 189)

Esna's Temple is located 50 km (30 mi) south of Luxor. It is dedicated to ***Khnum***, an Egyptian name that means *"moulder"*. He is usually shown as a ram-headed deity, fashioning people out of clay, at his potter's wheel.

The temple was begun by Ptolemy VI Philometer on the remains of a preceeding 18th Dynasty sanctuary, that was itself built over the ruins of earlier temples. The temple is situated about 9m (30ft) below the modern street level.

Originally, it must have been a typical full-fledged Egyptian temple. Everything vanished except the hypostyle hall, a forest of 24 columns. The columns are 13m (43ft) high, each fully decorated. Each column has a different capital, which imitates the shapes of flowers and plants. The ceiling has a very interesting rendering of the zodiac and astronomical scenes. The interior and exterior walls are also fully decorated.

Valley of the Upper Nile - Esna

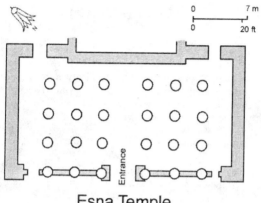

Esna Temple

Khnum, at his Potter's Wheel

El Kab (Nekheb)

(Location map on page 189)

El Kab is 26 km (16 mi) south of Esna. *El Kab* is the Arabic name of the ancient Egyptian *Nekheb*. *Nekheb* was the capital of this nome, whose vulture **netert**(*goddess*), **Nekhbet**, was the symbol of Upper Egypt. The figure of **Nekhbet** is found everywhere, either alone or together with **Uatchet**, the cobra (or uraeus) symbol of the North.

Vultures are known to be zealous in caring for their young, and are reputed as having no male of the species. The female vulture impregnates herself by exposing herself to the winds, i.e. **neteru**(*gods*), which metaphysically is a *virgin impregnation*.

The vulture represents primordial reconciliation. Reconciliation is also a feminine aspect of the universe, which is the reason that Egyptian women are shown wearing a vulture headdress.

Nekheb's remains are about 6000 years old.

Some points of interest include:

• The ruins of the main temple of *Nekhbet*, which was probably begun before 2700 BCE. It was continually enlarged considerably by several kings, including Tuthomosis III, Amenhotep II and the Ramessids.

• A chapel, originally built during the reign of Ramses II, which was restored by the Ptolemies, and is dedicated to several deities.

Valley of the Upper Nile - Nekheb & Nekhen   189

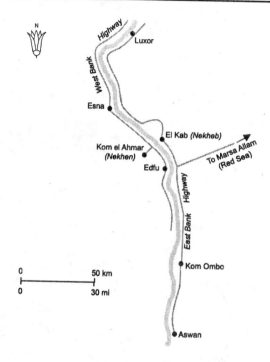

Kom el Ahmar (Nekhen)

(Location map above)

Nekhen is located west of the Nile. It is even older than *Nekheb*, as capital of the nome. Its Arabic name is *Kom el Ahmar*, or '*the red mound*'. This very ancient site includes tombs from pre-Dynastic Egypt to the New Kingdom.

Edfu

(Location map on page 189)

Edfu Temple is located 90 km (55 mi) south of Esna, and 110 km (70 mi) north of Aswan. Edfu's main attraction is its temple, that is dedicated to **Heru**(*Horus*), the falcon-headed **neter**(*god*). It is the best preserved of all Pharaonic temples. The temple plan is extremely homogeneous, and as such, it qualifies as the archetype of the Egyptian temple.

Ptolomy III began this temple in 237 BCE, and it took 200 years to complete. The present temple is a 2000 year old replica of the original early pharaonic design.

The main features of this temple include:

• **The entrance** to the temple is through a huge pylon, and is guarded by two beautiful granite falcons.

• **The Great Court** has a colonnade of 32 columns, on three sides, and is covered with beautiful reliefs.

• **An Antechamber**, that contains 18 columns. There are another two majestic black granite statues of the falcon **Heru**, wearing the double crown of Egypt, at its entrance.

• **A Hypostyle Hall** containing 12 columns, fully decorated.

• **Two fully decorated Antechambers**, beyond the Hypostyle Hall.

• **The Sanctuary of Heru**(*Horus*) is encircled with ten chapels.

• **All interior and exterior walls** are fully decorated with symbolic representations.

• **The Mammisi**(*Birth House*) is located near the temple, and depicts the usual divine(spiritual) birth.

Valley of the Upper Nile - Edfu

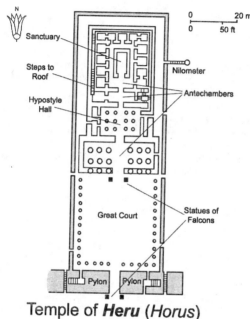

Temple of **Heru** (Horus)

Several important festivities occured here, among them:

1) The divine birth of **Heru**(Horus) at the Mammisi. Each pharaoh celebrated this event here, to symbolise his oneness with **Heru**(Horus).
2) the victory of **Heru**(Horus) over **Set**(Seth).
3) the annual visit of **Het-Heru** from her shrine in Dendara.

Kom Ombo

(Location map on page 189)
Kom Ombo is 50 km (30 mi) south of Edfu, and 40 km (25 mi) north of Aswan**(Sunt)**. *It is largely populated with Nubians, who were relocated here, before their lands were covered by the encroaching waters of Lake Nasser, south of* Aswan**(Sunt)**.

Kom Ombo's main attraction is its dual Temple of the crocodile-headed *Sebek*, and the falcon-headed ***Heru-ur**(Haroeris)*. It is a double purpose, symmetrical temple. The temple was begun by Ptolemy VI Philometor and other Ptolemies and Romans added to, and completed it.

The Main Features of the Site Include:

• There are double entrances, courts, colonnades (in a ruined state), hypostyle halls, and santuaries.
All interior and exterior walls, as well as all the remaining columns, are fully decorated with beautiful hieroglyphs and symbolic representations.

• On the outer corridor wall of the temple is a box of surgical instruments, carved in relief. The box includes metal shears, surgical knives, saws, probes, spatulas, small hooks and forceps.

• South of the main temple is the Roman Chapel of ***Het-Heru**(Hathor)*, which is now used to keep a large collection of mummified crocodiles, that came from a nearby cemetery, since the Roman times.

• The ruins of the Mammisi (the Birth House) is located outside the main pylon, and served as the usual divine(spiritual) birthplace of *Heru*.

Valley of the Upper Nile - Kom Ombo

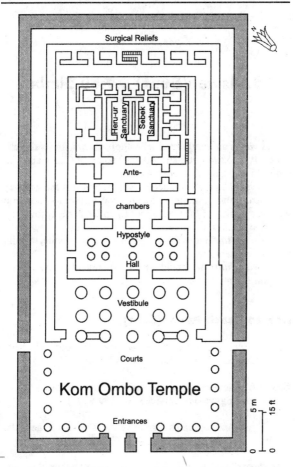

13. *Aswan(Sunt)* & Abu Simbel

Aswan is an interlude of relaxation, known for its dry climate. It is located 965 km (600 mi) south of Cairo, and 185 km (115 mi) from *Luxor*(***Ta-Apet***).

Aswan is Egypt's southernmost city, and it is the gateway to Africa. In ancient times, the area was known as ***Sunt***, and was then capital of the first Upper Egyptian nome (province). *Aswan* is its Arabic name.

Aswan(***Sunt***) provided the country with its granite, to build the ancient temples.

Aswan(***Sunt***) has grand sites from ancient times, as well as from the modern era.

How to Reach *Aswan*(Sunt)

Train - sleeper, air-conditioned wagons, 16 hours trip from Cairo. Contact: Wagons Lits (Tel: 349 2365, 761 319).

Bus - "*Golden Arrow*": air-conditioned super-jet buses. Contact: Upper Egypt Bus Service (Tel: 360 9307).

Air - *Egypt Air* - operates regular services to Aswan and Abu Simbel. (Tel: 245 4400, 390 2444, Cairo).

Nile Vessels - Nile trips, 4-6 days, organised by travel agents.

Aswan (*Sunt*) 195

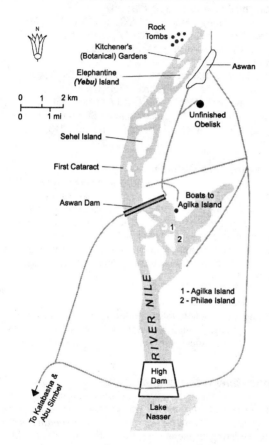

Around Aswan

Accommodations (Major Places)
Pullman Cataract Hotel *****, Sahara City (Tel: 323 222)
Hotel New Cataract *****, Abtal Al Tahrir St. (Tel: 323 434)
Hotel Oberoi Assuan *****, Philae Island (Tel: 323 455)
Amun Village *****, Sahara City (Tel: 480 438)
Hotel Amun Tourist ****, Amun Island (Tel: 322 555)
Hotel Isis ****, Al Nil Street (Tel: 326 891)
Hotel Kaiabsha ****, near Hotel Cataract (Tel: 322 999)
Hotel Cleopatra ***, Saad Zaghloul St. (Tel: 322 983)
Youth Hostel, Abtal Al Tahrir St. (Tel: 322 313)

The Unfinished Obelisk
(Location map on page 195)

At the edge of the northern granite quarries, lies a huge 43m (137ft) long fractured obelisk. It would have been the largest single piece of stone ever, if a flaw had not appeared in the granite. It is estimated to weigh 1,170 tons. So it lies there, with no inscription indicating its owner or intended purpose. You can see quarry marks around this obelisk.

Nile Feluccas
Many tours include felucca rides, to view the spectacular scenes of granite formations along the Nile banks, as well as a stop at the Botanical Gardens or *Elephantine(Yebu)* Island.

Elephantine(Yebu) Island
(Location map on page 195)

Elephantine(Yebu) Island was the location of the main town in ancient ***Sunt*** (present Aswan). *Elephantine* is the Greek rendering of the ancient Egyptian word, *Yebu,* which means both '*elephant*' and '*ivory*'. Excavation of the ancient town, which began at the start of this century, is still going on and the remains of the fortress and three temples are visible. *Yebu* was the worship/study centre of the ram-headed creator of humankind, Khnum, *neter*(*god*) of the cataracts, and his companion *netert*(*goddesses*) *Anket*(*Anukis*) and *Satet*(*Satis*).

You can visit the ruins of the ancient town, a museum, and the Nilometer. There are also ruins of several stone temples from various periods, such as the remains of a large temple built by Nectanebo, a 4th century BCE pharaoh, which is dedicated to Khnum. Nearby are the remains of a small portion of the Temple of *Satet*(*Satis*).

Sehel Island

(Location map on page 195)

Sehel has many sites that were dedicated to *netert*(*goddess*) *Anket*(*Anukis*) and her consort, Khnum.

An important stele, located on the southeastern side of the island, records the story of a seven year famine that plagued Egypt during the much earlier time of Pharaoh Zoser. The stele is dated to about 200 BCE. It is a copy of an Old Kingdom text, which dates to the reign of Zoser, 2500 years earlier. It is commonly known as the *"Famine Stele"*.

The three main characters on the stele, are Khnum (who represents the Divine Principle of Molding), King Zoser and Imhotep. This stele should have been named *Khnum's Alchemical Stele*, for it holds the key to the method of manufacturing man-made stone. Approximately one-third of this stele's content pertains to rocks and mineral ore, and their processing. There are references to making stones on this stele. Columns 18 and 19 of this Stele quote the Divine Molder, Khnum, speaking to King Zoser:

"I am Khnum, your creator, ... I give you rare ore

after rare ore .... Never before has anyone processed them (to make stone) in order to build the temples ....".

Botanical (Kitchener's) Gardens

(Location map on page 195)

Mid-stream, near *Elephantine(Yebu)* Island, is a natural exhibition of equatorial and tropical trees and shrubs. This island was given to Lord Kitchener in the 1890s when he was council-general of Egypt and commander of the Egyptian army. He imported plants from the Far East, India and other parts of Africa, to form these beautiful gardens.

The Rock Tombs

(Location map on page 195)

These rock tombs are located on the west bank of the Nile. They are the tombs of the princes, governors, and other dignitaries of the Old and Middle Kingdoms. They are mostly unimpressive, except a few that may be worth visiting.

The Temple of Kalabsha

(Location map on page 195)

Located 10 km (6 mi) south of the High Dam on the west bank of the lake, this temple is dedicated to **Merur**(*Mandalis*), a form of the sun-neter. Dating back to the Roman Emperor Octavius Augustus (30 BCE - 14 CE), the temple was moved from its original site 55 kms (34 mi) south of Aswan, on the west bank, and rebuilt near the High Dam. It is one of the largest sandstone temples in the area. Its walls are covered with texts and inscriptions depicting Egyptian deities such as **Auset**(*Isis*), **Ausar**(*Osiris*) and others.

The Aswan Dam

(Location map on page 195)

This dam was built between 1898 and 1902. It was raised twice in later years. However, it did not provide the protection or the demands for more agricultural lands and electricity. Now, it is completely surpassed in function, by the much larger High Dam, situated 6 km (4 mi) upstream.

The High Dam

(Location map on page 195)

The Aswan High Dam was completed in 1964, and is located 6 km (4 mi) south of the old dam.

It was built to safeguard Egypt against the high Nile floods, which either destroyed large tracts of land or ran wastefully into the Mediterranean. The dam, 111m (365ft) above sea-level, is 3,600m (2.2 mi) long and 40m (131ft) wide at the top, and 4 km (2.5 mi) across.

The water stored behind the dam has created the 500 km (300 mi) long Lake Nasser, the world't largest artificial lake. The rising level of this lake has forced the relocation of thousands of Nubians and Sudanese, south of Aswan.

The High Dam controls and regulates the fluctuation of the flow of the Nile at all times. As a result, the area of Egypt's cultivable land was increased by 30%, and the High Dam's hydroelectric supply has doubled Egypt's power output.

A few years ago, when central and eastern Africa was suffering from lack of rain and famine, Egypt was not affected, mostly because the stored water behind the dam, during the rainy years, was utilized during the dry years.

On the other hand, artificial fertilisers now have to be used because the dam hinders the flow of silt, that was critical to the Nile Valley's fertility.

Auset(Isis) Temple of Ancient Philae

(Location Map on page 195)

This ancient temple, that was originally located on Philae, is now relocated on Agilka Island. It was repositioned, to correspond as closely as possible to its original location. More about the reasons, and its related history, after describing the temple.

The main features of this temple complex include:

• **The First Pylon** - which has beautiful wall carvings.

• **The Great Court**, with 31 (was originally 32) beautiful columns with various floral capitals on the west side, and six columns on the east side.

• **A small temple,** dedicated to Imhotep, at the rear of the eastern colonnade.

• **The Central Court**, which inclues a *Mammisi(birth-house)*, dedicated to *Heru(Horus)*. At the northeast corner of the Court, is a building that was used as a healing centre.

• **The Second Pylon**, - which has intruiging depictions, in its carvings. It also provides access to the Vestibule and the Inner Sanctuary.

• **The Temple of *Het-Heru(Hathor)***, east of the second pylon, is beautifully decorated.

• *Ausar(Osiris)* **Chambers**, can be reached via a staircase at the western side of the second pylon. The Chambers are fully decorated with beautiful images of *Ausar(Osiris)*, *Auset(Isis)*, and other deities that took part in the *Ausar(Osiris)* and *Auset(Isis)* Legend.

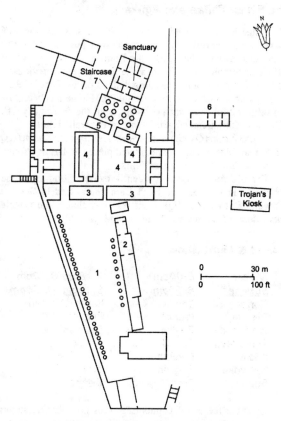

Temple of Ancient Philae

The Sites: Philae and Agilka

Philae is pronounced 'feel-ay'. Philae was the home of *Auset(Isis)* Temple. This temple was begun under the Ptolemies, and finished under the Romans, in the 3rd century CE. This temple was built on a site that was used previously, and its Egyptian name, meaning "Island of the Time of Ra", suggests an extremely remote antiquity. Philae has been luring pilgrims for thousands of years, until the 6th century CE. The early Christians defaced some of the wall reliefs.

In the *Ausar(Osiris)* and *Auset(Isis)* legend, *Auset(Isis)* while searching for the dismembered pieces of *Ausar(Osiris)*, found her husband's heart on Philae.

The old Aswan Dam frequently caused flooding of the temple in Philae, but the High Dam guaranteed to flood it forever. Before the High Dam was completed, the temple was relocated on nearby Agilka Island.

Sound & Light Show

	Winter	*7:15pm*	*8:30pm*
	Summer	*9:15pm*	*10:30pm*
	6:00pm / 8:00pm		
Monday	English	Italian	Italian
Tuesday	French	English	
Wednesday	English	Spanish	French
Thursday	French	Arabic	
Friday	English	French	
Saturday	English	French	
Sunday	French	German	

Entrance fee is EP30 plus EP3 sales tax. Private shows for a minimum of 50 people, are available with prior arrangement. Contact: Misr Co. for Sound & Light, Cairo (Tel: 202 385 2880, 386 5469, Fax: 202 384 4259).

Auset(*Isis*): Beloved of All

Ancient Egyptians called her "*Auset* with the 10,000 names (attributes/qualities)".

Isis is the Greek rendering of the Egyptian '*Auset*'. *Auset*, in Egyptian means '*throne*'.

Many elements of the *Auset*(*Isis*) myth and the story of the Virgin Mary are very similar, for both were able to conceive without the male impregnation. *Heru*(*Horus*) was conceived and born after the death of *Auset*(*Isis*)'s husband, and as such, she was revered as the Virgin Mother.

Auset(*Isis*) is the power responsible for the creation of all living creatures.

Auset(*Isis*) is portrayed wearing the vulture headdress, the crescent and disk, with a pair of horns surrounding the disk. Sometimes she is shown in purely human form.

Auset(*Isis*) was related to the star Sirius, whose annual appearance ushered in the Nile's inundation and the Egyptian New Year.

Since *Auset*(*Isis*) had many names and forms, she was equated in the Greek mythology with Persephone, Ceres, and Athene.

She is the universal Mother of Nature, and protector of mankind. She was identified with all similar goddesses of the Mediterranean and Asia.

Her followers from all over the ancient world made their pilgrimage to her shrine in Philae, long after the establishment of Christianity throughout the Roman Empire.

Abu Simbel

Abu Simbel is located 275 km (170 mi) south of Aswan. It has two temples, which were built 3,200 years ago by Ramses II (1304-1237 BCE).

The Greater Abu Simbel Temple (Ramses II)

The first, and largest of the temples, is dedicated to the sun *neter*(*god*) Ra-Harakhte. The main features include:

1 - **The facade** is 33m (110ft) high, and 38m (125ft) broad, and guarded by four statues of Ramses II, each of which is 20m (66ft) high.

Between the legs of the colossal statues on the facade, there are smaller statues of Ramses II's family: his mother "Mut-tuy", his wife "Nefertari" and his sons and daughters.

2 - **The Great Hall of Pillars** is located beyond the entrance. It has eight pillars bearing Ramses II in the form of *Ausar*(*Osiris*). The wall and column reliefs here depict the victorious king, against his enemies.

Other side rooms are fully decorated with ceremonial representations.

3 - **The Holiest of Holies**, 55m (180ft) back into the living rock, where there are four sitting statues of: Ra-Harakhte, Ptah, Amen-Ra and King Ramses II.

The sun shines directly on the Holiest of Holies two days a year: February 22, the king's coronation date, and October 22. After the relocation of the temple, the dates are now February 23 and October 23.

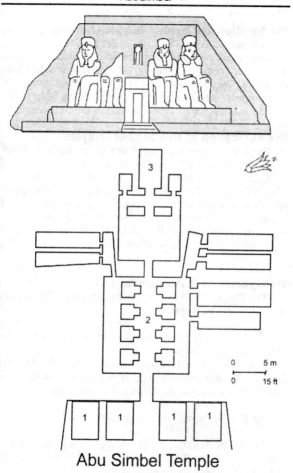

Abu Simbel Temple

The Smaller Abu Simbel Temple (Nefertari)

This temple is located a short distance from the main temple. It was carved in the rock and dedicated by Ramses II, to his beloved wife, Nefertari. The facade is adorned by six statues, four to Ramses II and two to his wife Nefertari, in the form of *Het-Heru(Hathor)*, *netert(goddess)* of Love.

The interiors look like the interior of the main temple.

The Relocation of Abu Simbel Temples

These two temples attracted worldwide attention when they were threatened by inundation by the rising waters of the High Dam. In response to an appeal by Egypt, In 1959, UNESCO initiated an international donations campaign to save these monuments. The rescue of the Abu Simbel temples began in 1963. To save it from inundation, the temples, weighing about 40,000 tons, were cut into 2,000 pieces, moved 28m (90ft) higher, and reassembled on a higher plateau.

Transportation & Accomodations

The 275 km (170 mi) trip from Aswan can be accomplished in several ways:

By Air: daily flights to Abu Simbel. Contact: Egypt Air (Tel: 245 4400 / 390 2444 in Cairo).

You could fly from Aswan and return back in the same day, or you may stay overnight at one of the nice hotels in Abu Simbel (Nefertari or Nobaleh Ramses Hotels).

By Bus: Air-conditioned daily buses.

By Taxi or Minibus: By getting a group together and hire a taxi or minibus. Seek the help of the information desk in your hotel, or your travel guide/agent.

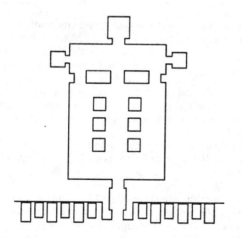

Het-Heru *(Hathor)* Temple
(Nefertari)

14. Alexandria

Alexandria is Egypt's second largest city, with a population of about 5.5 million. It lies about 220 km (136 mi) from Cairo. It gets more rain than Cairo, and therefore boasts more greenery, and a richer, cleaner appearance. It is sometimes referred to as the *"Pearl of the Mediterranean"*.

Today, Alexandria is a major industrial centre. The majority of Egypt's export and import trade goes through its port. The beaches of Alexandria are a favourite summer resort for Egyptians.

There isn't much of ancient Alexandria left to see. The ancient city is buried under the houses of the centre of the modern city.

Alexander the Great, in 332 BCE, founded the city of Alexandria, on the site of a small village called *Rhakotis*.

Alexander and the Ptolemies who followed him, agreed to protect the Egyptian borders, and to leave Egyptian ways as they were. In return, they governed Egypt, from the distant isolated (at that time) city of Alexandria.

One of the Seven Wonders of Antiquity, the Pharos Lighthouse, 140m (460ft) high, stood on the island with the same name, in front of the harbour. This island has been connected with the mainland, since antiquity, with a 1200m (3/4 mi) long dyke.

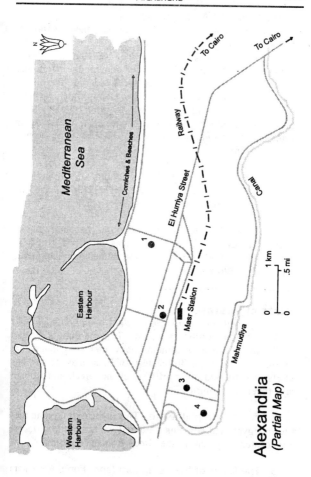

The Library of Alexandria was established under one of the early Ptolemaic rulers. The Ptolemies gathered hundreds of thousands of Egyptian manuscripts, which were collected from all over Egypt. It was then believed that the library would protect this Egyptian written knowledge, from any possible invaders. Not long after its foundation, the library was reputed to contain over 200,000 manuscripts, and later grew to 900,000. During the time of Julius Caesar, the library was burned down. It was rebuilt and restocked again during the Roman era, and burned again in 640 CE, leaving nothing behind.

The translation of the Old Testament into Greek, was done (the interpretation according to the Seventy) in Alexandria, during the Ptolemies' rule.

The Ptolemies ruled from Alexandria, practically out of touch with the people, until the Romans wrestled Egypt from Cleopatra VII, in 30 BCE. Under the Roman domination, the city continued to flourish.

Points of Interest
(Numbered in the same order on map on page 209)

1 - **Greco-Roman Museum** - This museum is located on El Mat-haf Street. It contains many interesting items, that go back as early as the 3rd century BCE, such as statues, bas reliefs, jewelry and other artifacts of the Greek and Roman days (over six centuries).

2 - **Roman Amphitheatre** - This is the only Roman theatre in Egypt, and contains 12 tiered white marble terraces. It is located very near to the Greco-Roman Museum.

3 - **The Ruins of the Serapeum (and "Pompey's Pillar)**

This once splendid Serapeum Complex, was built around 297 CE, for Diocletian (not Pompey). It originally consisted of an acropolis, topped by the Temple of Serapis (Serapis represented *Ausar(Osiris)*, when he took on the form of the bull as Apis), and several other shrines, along with a 25m (95ft) high with a circumference of 9m (30ft) pink granite pillar, commonly (but wrongly) known as Pompey's Pillar.

In about 391 CE, the Christians destroyed the Serapeum, leaving only the granite (Pompey) Pillar, some subterranean galleries, an *Auset(Isis)* temple, and a few statues.

The ruins of the Serapeum and the Pillar are located in a small park, about 2.5 km (1.5 mi) from the city's centre.

4 - The Catecombs of Kom el Shugafa - This is the most important underground Roman cemetery in Egypt. It is a maze of corridors, rooms, and tombs. The cemetery consists of three tiers, hewn out of the rocks at a depth of 30m (100ft). It dates back to the end of the 1st century, and the beginning of the 2nd century CE. Over 300 people were buried here.

• Beaches - The sandy beaches stretch over 40 km (25 mi). The beaches near the centre of Alexandria (Eastern Harbour to Montazah) are overcrowded. Beyond that, the beaches are cleaner, and more spacious.

• Corniche - It is a pleasant stroll along the Corniche, and in the evenings, you will find many lively nightclubs.

Accomodations & Transportation
• It is almost impossible to find accomodations in Alexandria in the summer, especially in August. As in Cairo, you can find live music and discos in most of the major hotels.
• You can get there by air (EgyptAir), train, bus, service taxis, or cars.

15. The Mediterranean Coast

The northern coastline, west of Alexandria, is undergoing several beach resort projects, along this beautiful 'Egyptian Riviera'. Going west from Alexandria, you will encounter:

• **Sidi Kreir Beach**, 34 km (21 mi) west, has a tourist village and a casino.
• **Ikingi Mariut**, 35 km (22 mi) west, is noted for therapeautic tourism and duck shooting.
• **Abu Mena District**, 50 km (31 mi) has some ancient buildings and churches, that date back to the early centuries.
• **Borg el Arab Area**, 52 km (32 mi) contains the temple of Abu-Sir, and a collective tomb from the Roman era. Nearby, is the Marakeys Tourist Village, considered one of the largest on the Northern Coast. It contains all the amenities, including chalets, villas, and flats.

• **El Alamein**, located 105 km (65 mi) west of Alexandria, is the site of the battle between the Allied (field Marshall Montgomery) and the Axis forces (Field Marshall Rommel) during WW II. El Alamein also offers a Tourist Village, with all the amenities for a relaxing summer vacation.
• **Sidi Abdel-Rahman**, 127 km (79 mi) west, is situated on a quiet bay, and boasts dry air, clear waters, and fine white sandy beaches, as well as villas and tourist camp.
• **Marsa Matruh**, is a major city, 288 km (178 mi) west, and boasts clean white sand beaches.

The Mediterranean Coast

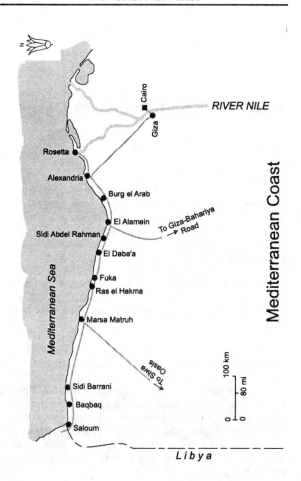

16. The Egyptian Sahara Oases

The most inhabited oases (depressions) of the Egyptian Sahara are: El Fayoum, Bahariya, Farafra, Dakhla, Kharga, and Siwa.

El Fayoum, near Cairo, is so close to the Nile, that people forget they are in an oasis. The other five depressions to the west, comprise about 1% of Egypt's total population.

Bahariya and Farafra Oases are accessible from Cairo.

Dakhla and Kharga Oases are best accessed from the city of Asyut.

Siwa Oasis, to the far west of Egypt, is closest to the city of Marsa Matruh, along the Mediterranean coast.

The five oases to the west (Bahariya, Farafra, Dakhla, Kharga, and Siwa), require lots of good planning, time, and money to visit. You are better off to consult with a knowledgeable travel agent, who specializes in travel through deserts and to oases. Find out where you are going to stay, accomodation, food services, transportation, if the sites that you wanted to see are open, ...etc.

The Egyptian Sahara Oases

Western Oases

El Fayoum Oasis

El Fayoum Oasis is about 100 km (65 mi) southwest of Cairo, and is Egypt's largest oasis. It has a population of about 2 million. It lies below sea level, and contains Lake Qarun, a popular lake for fishing and bird hunting.

This area is very fertile, and rich in agricultural produce, such as cotton, sugarcane, olives, rice, oranges, etc. A large percentage of Egypt's rose oil (essence) comes from here. The city of El Fayoum is the major city in the oasis, and is highly populated.

Lake Qarun occupies about 1/5 of the El Fayoum Oasis, on the northwestern edge. The lake was originally used as a catchment basin for the Nile overflow, and once filled the entire region. This water carried with it, and deposited, the fertile Nile silt on the bottom of the lakebed, since the Middle Kingdom. In the 12th Dynasty, the flow of water into the lake was reduced. As a result, about 80% of the original lake area was reclaimed and the rich soil was cultivated.

The ancient Greeks believed the crocodiles in this lake were sacred, and termed the area 'Crocodilopolis'. They built a temple in honour of *Sebek*, the crocodile-headed *neter*(*god*). During the time of the Ptolemies, people made pilgrimages from all over, to feed the sacred crocodiles.

Points of Interest

• The remains of the Temple and Pyramid of Amenemhat III, which is known as Hawara Pyramid and Labyrinth, are located at Hawarat el Makta.

• Snefru's Pyramid of Meidum (more details on page 120).

• Qasr Qarun, a well-preserved temple of the Greco-Roman era.

• Lake Qarun for fishing, bird hunting, and relaxing.

Bahariya Oasis

This prosperous oasis is 330 km (205 mi) south of Cairo. The Bahariya Oasis Depression differs from the other depressions in the Western Desert in that it is surrounded by an escarpment.

The depression is 42 km (26 mi) long, and 14 km (8 mi) wide.

Dolorite and quartzite rock hills are scattered along the depression floor.

The Oasis contains several villages, with the major village being Bawiti, with a population of 30,000. Dates, olives, and turkeys are popular exports from this area.

Points of Interest
- A 17th Dynasty temple of Amen in Bawiti.

- There are several hot sulphur springs, a few kilometers north of Bawiti.

- Cold springs with a splash pool can be found a few kilometers southwest of Bawiti.

Transportation
You can take a bus or drive from Cairo. Service taxis are also possible, but rare.

Accomodations
- There are very few hotels and restaurants.
- Camping is possible in some locations.

Farafra Oasis

Farafra Oasis Depression is the smallest of all the Egyptian Oases. It is about 300 km (186 mi) from Dakhla, and 185 km (115 mi) from Bahariya.

Farafra is connected to Dakhla by a road that crosses the chalk escarpment at Bab al Qasmand Pass.

Qasr el Farafra, supported by 20 freshwater springs, is the major village in the depression.

There is a large area of sand dunes in the eastern and southeastern section of the depression which extends for some 150 km (93 mi).

Points of Interest
• The covered hot springs.

• The White Desert, about 40 km (25 mi) from the village, is a region of white sand and interesting rock formations.

Transportation
You can reach Farafra Oasis by driving or bus, from either Dakhla or Bahariya Oases.

Accomodations
• There are very few hotels and restaurants.
• Camping is possible in some locations.

Dakhla Oasis

Dakhla Oasis Depression is 200 km (124 mi) west of Kharga, and 310 km (192 mi) southeast of Farafra. Unlike all of the other depressions, 45% of its land is cultivable.

Its primary water source is furnished by more than 600 deep artesian wells, supplied by rainfall in Equatorial Africa, which is believed to take 500 years to reach this oasis.

Mut is the largest town in the oasis. El Qasr is also another town of interest in the area.

Points of Interest
- The hot sulphur pools in this area, between Mut and El Qasr, are known for their healing properties. Chalybeate Springs has a temperature of 35°C (95°F).

- Tombs, dating back to the 22nd century BCE, southwest of El Qasr, near the village of Amhada, as well as some colourful tombs from the Roman times.

- Amen Temple at Deir al Hagar.

Transportation
It takes three hours to drive by car/service taxi from Dakhla to Kharga. Buses are also available from the Kharga and Farafra oases.

Accomodations
- There are very few hotels and restaurants.
- Camping is possible in some locations.

Kharga Oasis

Kharga Oasis Depression is 230 km (142 mi) southwest of the Nile Valley town of Asyut. North to south, the depression is 185 km (115 mi), east to west 15-30 km (9-18 mi). Kharga Oasis has a population of 100,000. It's main town is El Kharga. One of the most distinctive features of the Kharga Oasis Depression is the escarpment that one must descend before arriving at the town of El Kharga. Evidence of tectonic plate movement can be seen in the escarpment walls.

Points of Interest
- The Nadura Temple, dating back from the time of Antonius Pius, in 138 CE.
- Temple of Amen at Hibis, which dates to the 6th century BCE.
- In the centre of the oasis is Kasr El Gueweka with a sanctuary dedicated to Amen.
- Further south is Baris, a temple consecrated to *Auset*(*Isis*) and Serapis.
- Kharga's duck farms and palm groves.

Transportation
By Air: EgyptAir, from Cairo and Luxor, as well as Air Sinai from Cairo.
Bus: There are several buses a day from Cairo to Kharga, via Asyut.
Taxi: A service taxi from Asyut, takes about three hours.

Accomodations
- There are few hotels and restaurants.
- Camping is possible in some locations.

Siwa Oasis

Siwa Oasis is located 300 km (190 mi) southwest of Marsa Matruh and 550 km (340 mi) west of Cairo.

The Siwa Oasis Depression has the saltiest water of all oases. Although this water comes from Equatorial Africa, the water passes through salty strata on its long journey north to Siwa. The entire floor of the depression is below sea level. The area of the oasis is 1,099 sq km (680 sq mi). The southern part of the depression is covered by a sea of sand.

The oasis is loaded with palm trees, olive trees, and fruit orchards. It also boasts hundreds of freshwater springs and streams, and a rich bird population.

Points of Interest

- The 26th dynasty Temple of Amun is located a short distance from the town of Siwa. Alexander the Great came to this place in 331 BCE, to search for the Oracle of this temple.

- Other archaeological diggings are taking place in the area.

Transportation

Siwa can be reached from Marsa Matruh, by bus, minibus or service taxi.

You can rent a bicycle or hire a careta (donkey cart), to get around the oasis.

Accomodation

- There are several hotels and restaurants.
- Camping is possible, near one of Siwa's freshwater springs.

17. The Red Sea

The Red Sea is 1,932m (1,207ft) long from north to south, 306 km (191 mi) from east to west, and 2,359m (7,785ft) deep. Cutting through the Gulf of Aqaba from the Dead Sea and continuing south through the Red Sea and on into East Africa, is the Great Rift Valley, the juncture of the African and Arabian Tectonic plates. The Red Sea is highly saline with small tides and exquisite coral shelves and reefs.

A virtual paradise for diving enthusiasts, the Red Sea is recognized by experts as the best dive site in the world. A myriad of exotic species of tropical reef fish, hard and soft unique coral formations and beautiful desert, add to the charm of the Red Sea.

Hurghada (Ghardaka)

Hurghada (Ghardaka in Arabic) is located 380 km (237 mi) south of Suez. This isn't the place for discovering the glory of ancient Egypt. It is strictly for a seaside vacationing. The water is a brilliant turquoise, and the snorkelling and scuba diving are among the best in the world.

Marine Museum
A few km north of town is a nice marine museum, with a good collection of colourful fish and sharks.

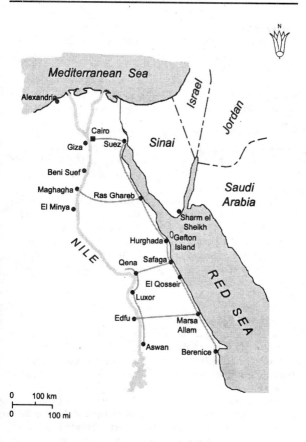

Red Sea Coast

Water Activities

Most of the good reefs are offshore, with Geftun Island being the most popular location. When planning a diving excursion, be sure to work with your hotel, or a local place that specializes in this. There are various trips that can be arranged, such as a day trip, which includes visiting two diving sites, and a lunch on Geftun Island, or a shorter trip to the 'House of Sharks', with no food included. Overnight trips are available too, with a night on Geftun Island - bring your own sleeping bag. Longer trips can also be arranged.

All kinds of water activities, such as diving, snorkelling, wind surfing, ...etc. are available. Glass-bottom boat rides are also offered.

Hotels and tourist villages are fully equipped and staffed, for all types of water activities. Swimming and relaxing along the beaches are also possible in most areas.

The standard cautions for any water recreation apply here too - protect yourself from sunburn, and protect your feet from the sharp coral. Also be wary of the dangers of some of the sea life.

Submarine Ride

For those of you who shy away from water sports, an easy way to view some of the underwater life, is a delightful trip in a submarine. It may seem a bit expensive, but you have to think about how much it must cost to keep the submarine running in good order. Your hotel can give you information on how to make reservations, and arrange transportation.

You leave your hotel or tourist village, and a bus takes you to the harbour, followed by a short boat ride to a floating platform. From here, you board a small submarine, with windows along each side, and submerge for about 45 minutes. It provides a superb view of underwater life.

Safari Trips

Safari trips to the desert are regularly available. Check with your hotel for details.

Accomodations

• There are numerous excellent hotels and self-sustained tourist villages, with all amenities for the whole family. There is excellent food, entertainment, and recreational activities for the whole family, at all these places.

• Camping is also possible in some areas.

Transportation

By Air: Daily flights from Cairo to Hurghada, via Egyptair and Sinai Air.

By Bus: There are frequent buses to and from Cairo every day. Buses are also available between Hurghada and both Qena and Luxor.

By Service Taxi: From Hurghada to Luxor - four hours; Aswan - six hours; Suez - four hours; Cairo - five hours.

By Boat: The Moreen II sails from Hurghada to Sharm el Sheikh three times a week. Check with your hotel and/or travel agent for reservations and ticket purchases.

Safaga

Safaga, 52 km (32 mi) south of Hurghada, is a small resort. It's main function is an export port of phosphates, from local mines.

Hotel accomodation and/or camping are available.

El Qosseir

El Qosseir is 85 km (53 mi) south of Safaga. It has areas for good snorkelling, along the beach.

18. Sinai

The Sinai peninsula is bounded by the Gulf of Aqaba on the east and the Gulf of Suez on the west. It is 61,000 sq km (23,500 sq mi) in area (6% of Egypt). It consists of a sandy desert in the north, and rugged mountains in the south. The mountains range from 750 to 2,500m (2460 to 8200ft). Its highest mountain peaks are Mt. Catherine at 2,642m (8,720ft), and Mt. Sinai at 2,285m (7500ft).

Sinai, is a region of awesome and incredible beauty, with interesting rock formations, wildlife, and the best underwater life man can experience. The quarries of Sinai have provided Egypt with enormous quantities of turquoise, copper, oil, and other minerals, since early Pharaonic times.

Hammam Fara'un (Suez Gulf)

It is an Arabic term, which means '*Pharaoh's Bath*'. It is a good resort and a rheumatism treatment centre. It has several hot springs, streams, and a nice beach.

Water Activities

Sharm El Sheikh, Dahab, Nuweiba, and Taba are four dive resorts, with several dive sites, which have clean and comfortable accommodations and are fully-equipped with dive centres, run by professional diving instructors.

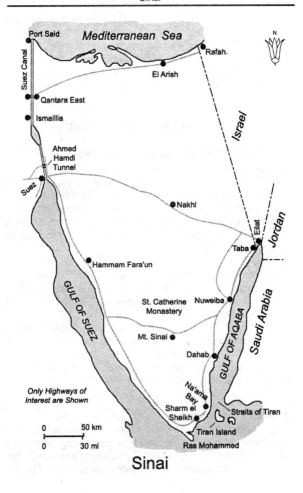

Na'ama Bay, at Sharm El Sheikh, is the largest and most active of these diving sites, and offers a fully equipped diving emergency centre with decompression chamber.

Masks, snorkels, and scuba gear are available. The diving centres also hire out windsurfers, kayaks, and paddle boats by the hour. Glass-bottom boat rides are also available.

The Coast of Aqaba Gulf

1 - Sharm El Sheikh and Na'ama Bay

The southern coast of the Gulf of Aqaba, between Tiran Island in the straits and Ras Mohammed at the southern tip of the Sinai, boasts a snorkelling and scuba diving paradise, considered to be among the best in the world. The water is crystal clear, the reefs fantastic, the scenery indescribable. A wide variety of rare and exotic fish can be spotted darting among the colourful coral.

This is also a good place for beginners to experience this refreshing sport, as the reefs are easily accessible, and all the training and equipment that you will need is available. The guides and instructors are quite patient and enthusiastic about sharing the beautiful wonders of this area.

Na-ama Bay and Sharm el Sheikh provide a wide selection of restaurants, bars, public services, and accomodations. Sharm el Sheikh and Na'ama Bay area contain mostly four and five star accomodations. You won't find much for the budget-minded, but prices are still affordable.

2 - Ras Mohammed

Ras Mohammed is located at the southernmost point of the Sinai, and is famed as one of the best diving sites in the world. They are trying to protect the beauty and natural life in this area, and as such, they regulate the number of people diving there, at any one time. It is now an environmentally protected area, called Ras Mohammed National Park. The beautiful coral gardens offer sightings of an incredible array of fish, in unbelievable colours and shapes. Your senses will be overwhelmed. Sharks can be found in this particular area, but generally keep to themselves. The water is deep here, so beginning swimmers might want to practice in shallow areas, until they are comfortable, before venturing to Ras Mohammed.

The park has a large variety of wild animals and birds, as well as interesting rock formations.

3 - Tiran Island

Tiran Island is a good site for diving, and is only accessible by boat. It is located in the Straits of Tiran, and has a strong current and higher shark population. It is beautiful, but Ras Mohammed is more popular.

4 - Dahab

Dahab, which means 'gold' in Arabic, is good location for the budget-minded tourist to enjoy some water sports. This beach resort is about 85 km (53 mi) north of Sharm el Sheikh, on the Gulf of Aqaba. You can see Saudi Arabia in the distance, across the water.

5 - Nuweiba

Nuweiba, 90 km (56 miles) north of Dahab, boasts some fantastic coral reefs and beautiful mountain scenery.

6 - Taba

Taba is the last resort on the Red Sea Coast of Sinai. Its geographic location allows views of Jordan, Saudi Arabia and Israel. If you are coming from Israel, you can obtain a special Sinai-only visa here, or from Egyptian consulates in Israel.

St. Catherine's Monastery

This monastery was built by Emperor Justinian I in the 6th century, at the foot of Mt. Sinai. It contains the Chapel of the Burning Bush, the Mosaic of the Transfiguration of Christ, and a library containing early Christian manuscripts. There are fifteen Greek orthodox monks living in this ancient monastery. The monastic order was founded in the 4th century CE by the Byzantine Empress Helena.

There are only a few parts of the monastery that are open to the public, including the chapel and a nice display of icons and jewelled crosses, as well as the fabled burning bush. Remember that this is still a functioning monastery.

Be careful when climbing the rocks on the outside. Unsuspecting tourists frequently slip and slide on the seemingly innocent landscape.

Mount Sinai (Gebel Musa)

The Monastery of St. Catherine is built at the base of Mount Sinai, which rises to a height of 2285m (7500ft). Gebel Musa is the local name of this mountain. There are two ways to climb to the top - a camel trail, and the 3750 Steps of Repentance, built by one of the monks. The camel trail takes about two hours, and is the easier choice. If you want to try the steps too, take them down rather than up, for an easier time. If you want to see the sunrise at the top, it's best to start your hike around 2 or 3am. Take a flashlight (torch), to help you see the trail. You can also make arrangements for an overnight trip, which offers camping on the mountain, and a splendid view at sunrise. Make sure you have plenty of food and water, and take along some warm clothes and sleeping bag, as it gets cold and windy there, with the high altitude, even in summer.

From the top of Mount Sinai, you can see the even higher Mount Catherine, which is the highest mountain on the Sinai

Peninsula, at 2642m (8720ft).

The Bedouins

There are 14 nomadic Bedouin tribes in Sinai, and they are one of the major attractions, for many of the travellers who visit this region. The Bedouins are a resilient and hospitable people, whose way of life goes back to the early centuries, although those who maintain the pure nomadic lifestyle are dwindling. Some of the Bedouins get involved in the tourist industry, by selling souvenirs, or organising camel trips to the interior of Sinai. There are also overnight treks to the Bedouin encampment at the Coloured Canyon, which is situated between St. Catherine's and Nuweiba.

Overland Exploration

Sinai's beautiful landscape can be explored by renting all-terrain-vehicles or 4-wheel-drives, or by taking a camel trek.

El Arish (Sinai Northern Coast)

El Arish, on the Mediterranean coast, is the capital of the northern region of the Sinai peninsula. It has a population of 50,000 people. It is reknowned for its calm waters, palm-shaded beaches and fine-grained white sand.

Transportation To Sinai

By Air: EgyptAir and AirSinai fly from Cairo to Sharm El Sheikh, St. Catherine, Taba, and El Arish.

By Bus: There are several buses between Cairo and Sharm El Sheikh, as well as connections between most Sinai destinations. The bus to and from Israel stops in El Arish.

By Service Taxi: They are available, but mostly connecting between Sinai major destinations.

Glossary

Amam - Composite beast. Symbol of the material world. Also see pages 174-176.

Ammit - see *Amam* (the Egyptian name).

Amen/Amun/Amon - means "Hidden", for he is everywhere, but you can't see him. He provides the spirit which animates the living earth and all creatures, and as such, he is the reason why the whole universe exists. In the creative aspect, he is identified with Ra, as Amen-Ra.

Anket - *Netert*(*goddess*) of the cataract region at *Sunt*(*Aswan*); consort of Khnum; represented as a woman with a high feather headdress.

Ankh - The symbol of eternal life. The Egyptian ankh emblem was the symbol of early Christians in Egypt.

Glossary

Anpu - Jackel-headed, patron of embalmers.

Anubis - See Anpu (Egyptian name).

Anukis - See *Anket* (the Egyptian name).

Apet/Opet - Hippopotamus *netert*(*goddess*), associated with pregnancy, gestation. and material creation.

Apis - the Greek name for *Hap* or *Hapi*, the sacred bulls. The Apis bull personified the sexual power/fertility of Ptah, creator of forms.

Aton - is the disk of the sun as the physical manifestation of Ra. Also see page 136.

Ausar - Ausar represents the mortal man carrying within himself the capacity and power of spiritual salvation. He came to earth for the benefit of mankind, with the title of "Manifester of Good and Truth". His death by the evil one was followed by his burial and resurrection, and then becoming the judge of the dead. *Ausar*(*Osiris*) was equivalent to Pluto and with Dionysos, in Greek mythology.

Auset(*Isis*) - the wife of **Ausar**(*Osiris*) and mother of **Heru**(*Horus*). Patron of one of the four canopic jars, protecting the liver. Also see page 203.

Ba - Ba is usually translated as the Soul. It is the divine, immortal essence. When the ba departs, the body dies. Ba is usually shown as a stork with a human head.

Bastet - Cat *netert*(*goddess*), the tame, aspect of Sekhmet. Also see page 122.

BCE - Before Common Era. Also noted in other references as BC.

Book of the Dead - consists of over a hundred chapters of varying lengths, which were mostly derived from the Unas Funerary (Pyramid) Texts. It is to be found, in its complete form, only on papyrus scrolls that were wrapped in the mummy swathings of the deceased, and buried with him.

Buto - See *Uatchet* (the Egyptian name).

Canopic Jars - Special jars used to store the vital organs of the deceased, The jars were placed in the tomb chamber near the mummy. The jars had lids

Glossary

shaped after the heads of the four sons of **Heru**(*Horus*), who were in charge of the protection and/or progression of the viscera. Each of the four sons was himself under the protection of a **netert**, and each was associated with one of the cardinal points. as follows:

Contents	Son	Netert	Head	Direct.
stomach	Duamutef	***Net****(Neith)*	jackal	north
intestines	Qebsennuf	***Serket****(Selkis)*	hawk	south
lungs	Hapi	***Nebt-Het****(Nepthys)*	baboon	east
liver	Amset	***Auset****(Isis)*	man	west

Cartouche - oblong figure which contains the name of royalties.

CE - Common Era. Also noted in other references as AD.

Djet/djed/djetta - See **Tet** (the Egyptian word).

Duat/Tuat - The Underworld, where the soul goes through transformation leading to resurrection.

Geb - the earth **neter**(*god*); consort of Nut; represented as a man, often reclining under Nut, the Sky **netert**(*goddess*).

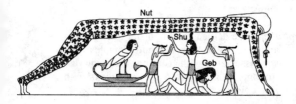

Haroeris - See ***Heru-ur*** (the Egyptian name).

Hathor - See ***Het-Heru*** (the Egyptian name).

Heb sed - Ancient festival associated with rejuvenation and spiritual and physical renewal, of the pharaoh.

Heru - is the falcon-deity, who is identified with the king during his lifetime. He is the son of ***Ausar****(Osiris)* and ***Auset****(Isis*. His centres are located in many places, e.g. Behdet in the Delta, and Edfu in Upper Egypt.

Heru-ur - He is ***Heru****(Horus)*-the-Elder. His temple is at Kom Ombo.

Het-Heru - is the provider of spiritual nourishment, pleasure, music, love, and dance. She is the consort of ***Heru****(Horus)*. Her main temple was at Dendara. The Greeks associated her with ***Aphrodite***.

Horus - see ***Heru*** (the Egyptian name).

Hypostyle Hall - hall in which the roof is supported by columns.

Imhotep - the deified chief minister of Zoser and architect of the Step Pyramid Complex. He was associated with learning, medicine, astronomy, etc. Equated by the Greeks with Asklepies.

Imouthes - See *Imhotep* (the Egyptian name).

Isis - see *Auset* (the Egyptian name).

Ithyphallic - With phallus erect. A sign of fertility.

Ka - A complex spiritual entity, that is often translated as the "personality". The ka does not die with the mortal body, but it reincarnates into another physical vehicle.

Khepri - A symbol for the transformational power of the sun. It is often represented as a beetle within the sun-disk. It is Ra, in his form of the scarab beetle.

Khnum - Ram-headed patron of Elephantine, the Cataract region, and of Esna. He moulded man from clay, on a potter's wheel. See illustration on page 187.

Khonsu - The third of the *Ta-Apet*(*Thebes*) Triad, Amen, Mut & Khonsu. He is associated with the moon, and as such, is elusive, a wanderer, and is associated with lunar functions, such as healing, childbirth, etc.

Lotus - white waterlily, that is likened to Egypt - the Nile Delta is the flower, and the Nile valley is the stem. The lotus was the symbol of Upper Egypt.

Maat - *netert*(*goddess*) of truth, right, and orderly conduct. The concept of Maat has permeated all Egyptian writings, from the earliest times and throughout Egyptian history. The concept by which not only men, but also the *neteru*(*gods/goddesses*) themselves were governed. She is represented as a woman with an ostrich-feather on her head.

Mastaba - is the Arabic word for 'bench'; a mud-brick, aboveground structure. Below the mastaba are the burial chambers of the deceased.

Min - Ithyphallic form of *Amen*, as a symbol of fertility. Also see page 138.

Mummification - The process was basically one of dehydration of the body, after the removal of the brain (through the nostrils), and the viscera (through an incision in the side of the body). The body is then packed with temporary material containing dehydrating and preserving agents, for forty days. The temporary packing is then replaced with permanent resin-soaked linens and fragrances. The body is then anointed and wrapped in fine linen gauze. It took seventy days to complete the process.

Mut - Consort of *Amen* of *Ta-Apet*(Thebes). Mut is usually depicted as a woman wearing a vulture headdress, sometimes she is shown with the body of the vulture. Mut can also be shown with feathered, outstretched winged arms, which matches our expression: 'under her wings'.

Glossary

Nebt-Het - sister of **Auset**(*Isis*). Acted with **Auset**(*Isis*) as mourner for **Ausar**(*Osiris*), and hence for other dead people. One of the four canopic jar patrons, protecting the lungs. Her name means 'golden/noblest/mistress (**Nebt**), of the place/house (**Het**).

Neith - See **Net** (the Egyptian name)

Nekhbet - vulture **netert**(*goddess*) of **Nekheb** (modern El-Kab); tutelary deity of Upper Egypt. Also see pages 188 & 125.

Nephthys - See **Nebt-het** (the Egyptian name).

Net - Patron of **Sau**(*Sais*) in the Nile Delta, represented as a woman wearing the red crown. Her emblem is a shield with crossed arrows. She is identified by the Greeks with Athena. One of the four canopic jar patrons, protector of the stomach.

Neter/Netert - Personification of divine principle. (god/goddess). Also see pages 64-67.

Nome - One of the 42 divisions/provinces or states of Egypt.

Nut - Personification of the sky as matrix of all. the sky-**netert**(*goddess*), consort of Geb, the earth-**neter**(*god*). Represented as a woman, her naked body, usually covered with stars, is curved to form the arch of heaven. She swallows the the sun, and it comes out the other end, to represent a cycle. See illustration on page 235.

Obelisk - monolithic stone pillar, with almost square sides tapering to a pyramidal top, which was used for astronomical purposes in ancient Egypt. Also see page 74.

Osiris - See ***Ausar*** (the Egyptian name)

Papyrus - plant that grows in Lower Egypt (Nile Delta), and acts as its symbol. The plant is used to make writing surface that is also called Papyrus, meaning "paper".

Ptah - Great creator ***neter***(*god*) of Men-Nefer(Memphis), the architect of heaven and earth. Patron of craftsmen, equated by the Greeks to Hephaestus. Also see page 104.

Ra - Ra is the solar principle, responsible for all creation. All ***neteru***(*gods*) who took part at the creation process, are aspects of Ra. Therefore, Ra is often linked with other ***neteru***(*gods*), such as Atum-Ra, Ra-Harakhte, etc.

Ra-Harakhte - a ***neter***(*god*) in the form of a falcon, embodying the characteristics of Ra and ***Heru*** (here called "***Heru*** of the Horizon").

Re - see ***Ra*** (the Egyptian name).

Glossary 241

Satet - *netert(goddess)* of the Island of Sehel, in the Cataract region, south of *Sunt(Aswsan)*. The daughter of Khnum and *Anket(Anukis)*.

Satis - See *Satet* (the Egyptian name).

Scarab - Amulet in the form of a black beetle, symbol of transformation. Also see Khepri.

Sebek - Crocodile-headed *neter(god)*, personifying the divine aspect of death, that is a necessity in order to achieve resurrection and eternal life; was revered as an aspect of Ra. Sebek temples can be found in Kom Ombo and El Fayoum.

Seker - Hawk-headed, with a swathed male figure; represents the deepest stage of the sun's journey beneath the earth (Duat). Saqqara is probably named after Seker.

Sekhmet - Lioness-headed consort of Ptah, and as such, represents the feminine aspect of the same creative power. Regarded as the bringer of destruction to the enemies of Ra.

Selkis - See *Serket* (the Egyptian name).

Serket - A *netert*(*goddess*), identified with the scorpion, which is renowned for its vigilance of caring for its young. *Serket* is usually shown as a woman with a scorpion on her head, or sometimes as a scorpion with a woman's head. She is one of the patrons of the four canopic jars, protecting the intestines.

Serapis - represented *Ausar*(*Osiris*) when he took on the form of the bull as Apis. Serapis is a combined *Ausar*(*Osiris*), Apis, and Zeus.

Serdab - hidden cellar in a tomb, containing a coffin with a painted statue of the deceased.

Sesheshat - A musical rattle sacred to *Heb-Heru*(*Hathor*).

Set - represents the power of opposition that is always working to prevent peace, harmony, and order. This opposition is necessary to maintain balance in the universe. *Set* and his accomplices represent the forces of darkness, chaos, etc. *Set* is identified with many animals, including the pig, ass, okapi, hippopotamus, etc. He is the brother of *Ausar*(*Osiris*), as well as his murderer. *Set* is the rival of *Heru*(*Horus*). He was equated by the Greeks with Typhon.

Seth - see *Set* (Egyptian name).

Glossary

Shu - personification of the air, or space, often shown as a man supporting ***Nut*** (sky), with ***Geb*** (earth) underneath.

Sistrum - see Sesheshat (Egyptian name).

Sobek - See Sebek (Egyptian name).

Sokar/Sokaris - See ***Seker*** (the Egyptian name).

Solar Barque/Barge/Boat - It was the symbolic vessel of transport, for the divine person's journey over the sea to final passage, to the eternal life.

Stele (plural: stelae) - stone or wooden slab or column decorated with commemorative inscriptions.

Tehuti - *Neter*(*god*) of wisdom and intellect. Also see page 131.

Tet - A symbolic pillar, representing the backbone of ***Ausar***(*Osiris*), the support of creation. It represents the channel through which the divine spirit might rise through matter to rejoin its source.

Thoth - see ***Tehuti*** (the Egyptian name).

Uatchet - The rearing cobra, a symbol for Northern Egypt. Also see pages 124-125.

Ushabti - A small figurine, usually of clay, buried with the mummy and charged with performing duties, on behalf of the deceased in the afterlife.

Selected Bibliography

Aldred, Cyril. *Egyptian Art*. London, 1990.

Erman, Adolf. *Life in Ancient Egypt*. New York, 1971.

Gadalla, Moustafa. *Egyptian Cosmology: The Absolute Harmony*. USA, 1997.

Gadalla, Moustafa. *Historical Deception: The Untold Story of Ancient Egypt*. USA, 1996.

Gadalla, Moustafa. *Pyramid Illusions: A Journey to the Truth*. USA, 1997.

Gadalla, Moustafa. *Tut-Ankh-Amen: The Living Image of the Lord*. USA, 1997.

Gardiner, Alan. *Egypt of the Pharaohs*. Oxford, 1961.

Herodotus. *The Histories*, tr. A. de Selincourt. New York and Harmondsworth, 1954.

James, T.G.H. *An Introduction to Ancient Egypt*. London, 1979.

Selected Bibliography

Lambelet, Edouard. *Gods and Goddesses in Ancient Egypt*. Cairo, 1986.

Lambelet, K. *How to Read Hieroglyphics*. Cairo, 1974.

Manniche, Lise. *Music and Musicians in Ancient Egypt*. London, 1991.

Montet, Pierre. *Eternal Egypt*, tr. Doreen Weightman. New York, 1964.

Murray, Margaret. *The Splendor That Was Egypt*. New York, 1972.

Osman, Ahmed. *The House of the Messiah*. London, 1994.

Osman, Ahmed. *Moses, Pharaoh of Egypt*. London, 1991.

Osman, Ahmed. *Stranger in the Valley of the Kings*. London, 1989.

Parkinson, R.B. *Voices From Ancient Egypt, An Anthology of Middle Kingdom Writings*. London, 1991.

Reeves, Carole. *Egyptian Medicine*. Britain, 1992.

Silverman, David P. *Language and Writing in Ancient Egypt*. Pittsburgh, 1990.

West, John A. *The Travelers Key to Ancient Egypt*. New York, 1989.

Wilkinson, Sir J. Gardner. *The Ancient Egyptians, Their Life and Customs*. London, 1988.

Index

A

Abtu(*Abydos*), 80, 179, 182, 185
  Temple of Seti I, 182-3
  Temple of Ramses II, 183
  Tomb of **Ausar**(Ausarion), 184-185
Abu Simbel, 204-207
Abydos, See **Abtu**
After-life, 175-177
Agilka Island, 195, 200-202
Akhenaton (formerly Amenhotep IV), 75, 132-137
  abdication, 137
  adopts Aton as 'father', 135, 136
  city of, See Tell el Amarna
  co-regency, 136-137
  father's death, 137
Akhetaton(city), see Tell el Amarna
Alexandria, 11, 28, 62, 208-211
Amarna (city), See Tell el Amarna
  kings, 132

  name, 132
Amen, 138, 146, 221, 232
  meaning, 141, 232
  processions of, 140-141
Amenhotep II,
  tomb, 156, 157
Amenhotep (*Amenophis*) III, 142-145, 148
  co-regency with Akhenaton, 136-7
  and Luxor Vanished Temple, 171
Amenhotep IV, See Akhenaton
Animals, entry requirements into Egypt, 35
Animal symbolism, 67, 124-125
Animal worship, 67
Ankh, 232
Anointing the king, 71
Anpu, 80, 175-6, 233
Anubis, See **Anpu**
Apet Festival, 140-1, 144, 146-7
Apet Temple at Karnak, 150
Apis, 113, 233
Arabic language, 12

Index

Aswan, 74, 194-9
Aswan Dam, 195, 199
Aswan High Dam, 195, 199
Asyut, 214, 215, 220
Aton/Aten, 136, 233
 and Akhenaton, 135-7
Ausar, 74, 233
 domain of, 80, 175-6
 Legend of, 79-80, 200-3
 resurrection, 79, 175-6
 temples of, 182-5
 tomb of, 184-5
 See also *Abtu*(*Abydos*)
Auset,
 Temple of Philae, 200-3
 and *Ausar*(*Osiris*), 79-80, 200-3
 and Sirius, 82-3
Aye, King, 132, 137

B

Ba, 234
Bahariya Oasis, 214, 215, 217
Baksheesh, 17
Bastet, 122, 234
Beni Hasan, 128, 129
Bent (southern) Pyramid of Snefru, 116-7
Book of Aker, 72, 110
Book of the Caverns, 72, 110
Book of the Coming Forth by Day, 72, 110, 131, 175, 234
Book of Day, 72, 110
Book of the Dead, See Book of the Coming Forth by Day
Book of the Gates, 72, 110
Book of Night, 72, 110
Book of What Is In the Duat, 72, 110
Bubastis, 122-3
Buto, See *Uatchet*

C

Cairo
 central, 87-9
 Giza, 86, See also Giza Plateau
 greater, 84-5
 modern, 84, 89
 pharaonic sites, 86, 88
Calendar, 74, 82-3, 179, 204-5
Canopic jars, 234-5
Carter, Howard, 160
Casinos, 41
Champollion, J. Francois, 68
Cheops, See *Khufu*
Chephren, See *Khafra*
Cleopatra, 62, 68, 180, 210
Cobra, symbolism of, 124-5
Coloured Canyon, 231
Coptic, language, 69
Cube
 symbol of universe, 81
 statues, 81
Cultural tips, See Chapter 2

D

Dahab, 226, 227, 229
Dahshur's Pyramids, 116-9
Dakhla Oasis, 214, 215, 219
Day of Judgment, 175-7
Delta, See Nile Delta
Deir el Bahari, See Hatshpesut Temple in Luxor
Deir el Medina, See Village of Workmen at Luxor
Demotic script, 68, 70
Dendera, **Het-Heru**(*Hathor*) Temple, 178-81
Deserts, See Egypt, geography, Western Oases, and Sinai
Diadem, 125
Djed-pillar, See **Tet**-Pillar
Djedefra, King
  pyramid of, 77
Dog Star (Sothis), see Sirius
Duat, 233, Also See Book of What is in the Duat

E

Edfu, 190
  Temple of, 190-1
Egypt
  economy, 15-6
  education, 16
  population, 13
  see individual topics in index, and Table of Contents

Egyptian Museum in Cairo, 86, 87
Egyptian Tourist Authority (E.T.A.), 23-7
El Alamein, 212-3
El Arish, 227, 231
El Fayoum, 214, 215, 216
El Kab, See Nekheb
El Minya, 128, 129, 130
El Quseir, 223, 225
Elephantine Island, 195, 196-7
Esna, 186, 189
  Temple of, 186-7

F

False doors, 106
Farafra Oasis, 214, 215, 218
Famine Stele, 197-8
Forty-two Assessors, 175-6, 182
Forty-two Negative Confessions, 175-7
Funerary texts, See Book of Aker, Book of the Caverns, Book of Day, Book of the Dead, Book of the Gates, Book of Night, Book of What is in the Duat

G

Gadalla, Moustafa, 1, 244
Gebel Musa, see Mt. Sinai

Index

Gebel Katrina, See Mt. Catherine
Gezirah Island, 85, 87, 89
Ghardaka, see Hurghada
Giza plateau, 86, 90-103
Gods, see *Neteru*
Great Pyramid of Giza, See Khufu Pyramid
Great Sphinx of Giza, 86, 91, 100-3
  physical site and construction, 100-2
  Temple of, 91, 97
  and *Khafra(Chephren)*, 100-2

H

Hammam Fara'un, 226, 227
Hathor, See *Het-Heru*
Hatshepsut,
  obelisk of, 76, 148-9, 151
  Punt, 162
  reign of, 164-5
  Temple in Luxor, 152-3, 162-3
  and Tuthomosis III, 76, 164-5
  and various temples, 168
Heb-sed, 236
Heb-sed festivals, 108, 149
Heliopolis, See *Onnu*
Hermetica (Hermetic Texts), 9
Hermopolis, See *Khmunu*
Herodotus, 9, 59, 122

Heru, 236
  and the *Ausar(Osiris)* Legend, 79-80, 203
  falcon of, 190, 192
  and *Het-Heru(Hathor)*, 179, 191
  Temple at Edfu, 190-1
  and *Set*, 80
Het-Heru, 236
  Temple at Dendara, 178-81
hieratic script, 68-70
hieroglyphs, 69-70
  deciphering of, 68-9
Horemheb, 132
Horus, See *Heru*
Hu (or Huni), Pyramid, 77
Hurghada, 222-5

I

Imhotep, 106, 197, 200-1, 236
Isis, see *Auset*
Islam, see religions, in modern Egypt
Ismailia, 126-7

K

Ka, 237
Kadesh (Syrian City), See Ramses II and battle of Kadesh
Kalabsha, temple of, 198
Karnak Temples, 139, 146-51

Festival Temple of
  Tuthomosis III, 147, 149
Hypostyle Hall, 147, 148
obelisks, 76, 148-9, 151
Pavilion of Sen-
  usert(*Sestostris*) I, 146,
  150
Triple shrine, 146-8
Kerdassa, 48
Kha-ba, pyramid of, 77
Khafra, king, 96
  pyramid of, 77, 91, 96-7
  pyramid temple, 91, 96-7,
    184
  and Sphinx, 97, 100-2
Kharga Oasis, 214, 215, 220
Khmunu (*Hermopolis* in
  Greek), 129, 130-1, 186-7
Khnum, 186-7, 237
  and Famine Stele, 197-8
  Temple of, 186-7, 197
Khufu, king, 92, 178
  at Bubastis, 122
  Great Pyramid of, 77, 91,
    92-5
  pyramid exteriors, 93, 95
  pyramid interiors, 92-4
  Boat Museum, 90, 95
  and Sphinx, 102
king, religious role of, 71-2,
  73
Kitchener's (Botanical) Island,
  195, 197
Kom el Ahmar (*Nekhen*), 189
Kom Ombo, 192
  temples of, 192-3

L
Lake Timsah, 126-7
Lake Nasser (High Dam),
  199
Language
  ancient, 68-70
  modern, 12, 62
Litany of *Ra*, 72, 110
Luxor/Thebes, 138-76
  East Bank, 139, 140-51
    museum of, 139, 140
    Temple of, 139, 142-5
      Birth Room, 144-5
      colonnade of
        Amenhotep III, 144
      Hypostyle Hall, 144
  West Bank, 152-76
    Temples/Tombs -
      Individual tombs and
      temples on West Bank
      listed under each's
      name.
    Tombs of the Nobles,
      152, 153, 172-3, 165
    Valley of the Kings, 152,
      153, 154-60, 165
    Valley of the Queens,
      152, 153, 161, 165

M
Maat, 175, 238
Mallawi (Mal-Levi), 130, 132
Man, as a symbol of the
  universe, 65, 81
Manetho, 59, 60
Marsa Matruh, 212-3

Mastaba, 108-9, 238
Mastabat Fara'un, 99, 114-5
Medinat Habu, See Ramses III Commemorative Temple
Mediterranean Coast, 212-3
Meidum, Snefru Pyramid of, 120-1, 216
Memnon, Colossi of, 153, 171
Memphis (*Men-Nefer*), 104, 106
Menes (*Mena*), 59, 60
Menkaura, king, 98
 pyramid of, 77, 90-1, 98-9
Min, 139, 238
Monotheism, in religion, 64-5
 and Akhenaton, 135-7
Mt. Catherine, 227, 230-1
Mt. Sinai, 227, 230-1
Mummification, 238
Mycerinus, See *Menkaura*

N

Na'ama Bay, 227, 228
Nebt-Het, 79, 239
Nefertari, Queen of Ramses II
 and Abu Simbel Temple, 206-7
 Tomb, 161
Nekheb, 188-9
Nekhen, 189
Nekhbet, 124, 125, 188

Nephthys, See *Nebt-Het*
Neteru ('*gods*'), 65, 66, 67, 73, 112-3, 239
 and Akhenaten, 135-6
New Valley, see Western Oases
Nile, the, See Egypt, Geography
Nile Activities, 23, 41, 43, 52-3, 56, 196
Nile Delta, 10, 122-4
Nuweiba, 29, 226, 227, 229

O

Oases, See Western Oases
Obelisks, 74, 76, 148-9, 151, 196, 240
Old Cairo, 85, 88
Onnu (*Heliopolis*), 85, 86, 88, 136
Oseirion, See *Ausarian*
Osiris, See *Ausar*

P

People of the Sea, 168, 169
Pepi II, King, 114
 pyramid of, 114-5
Pets, entry requirements into Egypt, 35
Pharaoh, 64, 71-2, 73, 125
Pharaonic Village, 86
Philae Island, 80, 195, 202-3
 Temple of *Auset*(*Isis*), 200-3
Philistines, See People of the

Sea
Port Said, 28, 126-7
Potters Wheel, 186-7
Pre-Dynastic Egypt, 58-60, 100-2
Ptah, 104, 240
Pyramid Age, 77, 99
Pyramid (Unas) Texts, 72, 110
Pyramids, 77, 86, 90-9, 105, 110, 114, 116-21
   as tombs, 78-9, 110-11, 114
   See also, individual pyramids

Q
Qadesh, See Kadesh
Qantara, 127, 226
Quseir, See El Quseir

R
Ra, 88, 176, 240
Ramses I tomb, 158, 159
Ramses II, 104, 113, 142, 148, 166, 182-5
   and Abu Simbel, 83, 204-7
   and Battle of Kadesh, 72, 142, 164, 204
   at Rammesseum, 152, 153, 166-7
   as usurper, 75-6
Ramses III, Pharaoh, 146-7, 149, 150, 188
   Commemorative Temple of (Medinat Habu), 152, 153, 168-70
Ramses VI tomb, 158, 159
Ramses IX tomb, 158, 159
Ramesseum, See Ramses II at Ramesseum
Ras Mohammed, 227, 228-9
Re, see *Ra*
Red Pyramid, Dahshur, 118-9
Red Sea Coast, 222-5
reincarnation, 176
Religion in ancient Egypt, 64-7
   and afterlife, 79-80
   animals in, 67
   centres of, 86, 88, 104, 130-1, 138
   gods, See *Neteru*)
   monotheism, 64-5
   myth and theology, 66
   and reincarnation, 176
   resurrection, belief in, 79, 80, 175-6
Religions, in modern Egypt
   Islam, 13-5, 62
   Christianity, 15, 62
   Judaism, 15
Roda Island, 85, 87
Rosetta stone, 68-9

S
Safaga, 223, 225
Saint Catherine's Monastery, 227, 230

Index

Sais, See *Sau*
Saqqara, 86, 106-15
  Enclosure Wall, 106, 108-9
  Mastabat Fara'un, 114-5
  Nobles' Tombs, 112-3
  Pepi II Pyramid, 114-5
  Persian tombs, 113
  Serapeum, 113, 210-11
  Step Pyramid of Zoser, 108-9
  Unas Pyramid, 110-11
  Zoser Pyramid Complex, 106-9
Sau, 123, 124, 239
Schwaller de Lubicz, R.A., 75, 142
Sehel Island, 195, 197-8
Sekhemket, pyramid of, 77
Serapis, 242
Serapeum, 113
Set, 242
  in the *Ausar*(*Osiris*) legend, 79-80
  and *Ausar*, 79
  and *Heru*(*Horus*), 80
Seth, See *Set*
Seti I, Pharaoh, 148
  Temples at *Abtu*(*Abydos*), 182-3
  Temple in Luxor's West Bank, 153, 166
  tomb of, 158-9
Sharm el Sheikh, 226-8
Sinai, 226-31
Sirius, 82-3
Siwa Oasis, 214, 215, 221
Snefru, King, 116, 118, 120
  pyramids of, 77, 116-21
Sphinx, See Great Sphinx
Step Pyramid, See Zoser Step Pyramid
Suez, 126-7
Suez Canal, 126-7
Symbolism, 66, 67, 73, 124-5, 152, 175-7, 182, 188

T

Taba, 28, 226, 227, 229
Tanta, 123, 124
Tehuti(*Hermes, Mercury*), 79, 130-1, 175-6
  and the Udjat-Eye, 80
Tehuti Research Foundation, 1, 23, 83, 256
Tell el Amarna, 129, 132-4, 137
  tombs at, 132-4
  see also Amarna
Tet pillar, 74, 243
Thebes, See Luxor
Thoth, See *Tehuti*
Tourist Information, 23-27
Tutankhamun, Pharaoh, 132, 144
  Tomb of, 154, 160
Tuthomosis III, Pharaoh, 104, 144, 149, 168, 188
  and Hatshepsut, 76, 149, 164-5
  accession, 164-5
  tomb, 156, 157
  as usurper, 76

U

Uatchet, 123, 124-5, 243
Unas, King, 110
   funerary texts of, 110
   pyramid of, 110-11
Utchat(Udjat) Eye, 80

V

Valley of the Kings, See Luxor, West Bank
Valley of the Nobles, See Luxor, West Bank
Valley of the Queens, See Luxor, West Bank
Village of Workmen at Luxor, 152, 153, 174-7
Vulture, symbolism of, 124, 125, 188

W

Weather, in Egypt, 12, 22, 37
Western Oases, 214-21
   See also individual oases
Women travelers, 19-20

Z

Zagazig, 122-3
Zoser, King, 78, 106, 197-8
   Step Pyramid Complex, 106-9
   Step Pyramid, 77, 78, 108-9
Zodiac of Dendera, 180

Maps

Abu Simbel Temples, 205, 207
Abydos Temples, 183
Alexandria, 209
Aswan
  Around Aswan, 195
  Temple of Anc. Philae, 201
Cairo
  Greater Cairo Area, 85
  Central Area, 87
  Giza Plateau (pyramids), 91
Delta, ancient sites, 123
Dendara, Temple of *Het-Heru*(*Hathor*), 181
Edfu, Temple of *Heru*(*Horus*), 191
Esna, Temple, 187
Egypt
  Overall Geographic, 11
  Internal Air Flights, 49
  Railways, 51
  Middle Upper, 129
  North of Luxor, 179
  Valley of Upper Nile, 189
Kom Ombo, Temple of, 193
Luxor
  East Bank, 139
  Karnak, Temples, 147
  Luxor Temple, 143
  Ramses III (Medinat Habu), 169
  Ramesseum, The, 167
  Temple of Hatshepsut, 163

Tomb of Amenhotep II, 157
Tomb of Ramses I, 159
Tomb of Ramses VI, 159
Tomb of Ramses IX, 159
Tomb of Seti I, 159
Tomb of Tutankhamun, 160
Tomb of Tuthmosis III, 157
Valley of the Kings, 155
Valley of the Nobles, 173
Valley of the Queens, 161
West Bank, 153
Mediterranean Coast, 213
Memphis area, 105
Pyramid Profiles
  Khufu(*Cheops*), 93
  Khafra(*Chephren*), 97
  Menkaura(*Mycerinus*), 99
  Snefru's Bent (Dahshur), 117
  Snefru's Red (Dahshur), 119
  Snefru's Collapsed (Meidum), 121
Red Sea Coast, 223
Saqqara
  Northern, 107
  Southern & Vicinity, 115
Sinai, 227
Suez Canal, 127
Tell el Amarna, 133
Western Oases, 215
Zoser Pyramid Complex, 109

About Tehuti Research Foundation

Tehuti Research Foundation is a non-profit international organization, dedicated to ancient Egyptian studies. Our books are engaging, factual, well researched, practical, interesting and appealing to the general public.

Visit our website at: **http://www.egypt-tehuti.com**

Ordering Information *(outside Egypt)*

Please send to:
Name _____
Address _____
City _____
State/Province _____ _____
Country: _____ Tel. (___) _____

___ Books @ $9.95 (Egyptian Cosmology)   = $___
___ Books @ $19.95 (Historical Deception)   = $___
___ Books @ $11.95 (Pyramid Illusions)   = $___
___ Books @ $9.50 (Tut-Ankh-Amen)   = $___
                                    Subtotal   = $___
  NC residents, add 6% Sales Tax   = $___
Shipping: (N.Amer. only) $2 for first book = $___
  each additional book $1 x ____   = $___
  Outside N.A.($8 per order, up to 5 bks) = $___
Total enclosed (check, m.o., Visa/MC/Disc) = $___

Bastet Publishing
P.O. Box 39406
Greensboro, NC   27438-9406, U.S.A.
E-Mail Address: USHorus@aol.com
Call TOLL FREE and order now   (888) 826-7021
Or FAX your order   (212) 656-1460